SpringerBriefs in Computer Science

For further volumes:
http://www.springer.com/series/10028

Urs E. Gattiker

Social Media Audit

Measure for Impact

 Springer

Urs E. Gattiker
CyTRAP Labs GmbH
Zurich, Switzerland
measure-for-impact@gmail.com

Additional book resources:
http://ComMetrics.com/
http://info.CyTRAP.eu

Measure for Impact:
http://My.ComMetrics.com

ISSN 2191-5768   ISSN 2191-5776 (electronic)
ISBN 978-1-4614-3602-7   ISBN 978-1-4614-3603-4 (eBook)
DOI 10.1007/978-1-4614-3603-4
Springer New York Heidelberg Dordrecht London

Library of Congress Control Number: 2012945000

Printed on acid-free paper

Springer is part of Springer Science+Business Media (www.springer.com)

Preface

Thank you for giving this book a chance. If you are reading this, you are at least thinking about picking up a copy. If you do, you are probably going to find something wrong with it despite my best efforts; nevertheless, I believe you will also find it an enjoyable way to spend a few evenings/weekends or commutes to and from work. Best of all, you will probably learn a few things along the line.

This book grew out of an introduction to social media assessment and benchmarking problems presented in various chapters previously published elsewhere. During our work and research at CyTRAP Labs GmbH, I began to develop a template for doing a social media audit, which evolved and became part of our *CyTRAP Social Media Audit Toolkit* (CySoMAT). We use CySoMAT to assess all social media activities, whether our own or those of our clients.

This work would not have been possible without the support of several people. I would like to thank all my colleagues, both near and far. Special thanks to Bryan Peters, Freydun Badri, and Christiane Stückelberger for acting as sounding boards, offering thoughtful suggestions, encouraging me to write down my thoughts, and being great colleagues and friends.

Thanks to Susan Lagerstrom-Fife, Jennifer Evans, and Jennifer Maurer at Springer for taking this project on and making the process a bit easier. Also thanks to Melanie Gattiker, editor extraordinaire; she often knows better than I do exactly what I am trying to say.

Finally, thanks to my wife, Verena, for putting up with my many quirks and long hours, particularly during the writing of this book.

Zurich, Switzerland   Urs E. Gattiker

Contents

Chapter 1
Introduction

Abstract This chapter provides a quick overview of what will be addressed in this book. In particular, the content of each chapter is summarized and, as importantly, how these things may apply to your work situation is discussed. Some critical questions and issues that must be addressed for social media use, whether beginning or continuing, are outlined. Examples are given throughout.

1.1 Motivation

My motivation for writing this book was two-fold:

1. I wanted to formalize ideas and processes I had been working on for a while.
2. Make this material accessible to more professionals for use in their work.

Of course, I did not expect that it would take as much time as it did. Nevertheless, the writing process helped me further refine my thoughts on this important topic. It also sharpened my own thinking regarding how social media influences our own social networking efforts, as well as the all important use of social media with in organizations.

Further, I received a lot of feedback from many clients, blog readers, and fellow researchers that helped me revise and improve the ideas and checklists presented in this book.

1.2 Who Should Read This Book

This book is intended primarily for *social media strategists, marketing and public relations professionals, as well as social media measurement folks*. It also includes materials for those simply interested in the topic but not all of the book's chapters will be equally interesting to a diverse audience. Finally, since you certainly do not

U.E. Gattiker, *Social Media Audit: Measure for Impact*, SpringerBriefs
in Computer Science, DOI 10.1007/978-1-4614-3603-4_1, © The Author(s) 2013

want to wade through six chapters to find the information pertinent to your job, *each chapter has a short introduction* to help you determine if you need to read further or move on to the next chapter.

1.3   Who Should Not Read This Book

Activities such as *building your own measurement tool from scratch, venturing far beyond the typical use of Web analytics and cost–benefit analysis* about anything state-of-the-art are not within the scope of this book. You will be really disappointed if you purchase this book because you want to do one of those things.

However, just because capturing the holy grail of semantic analysis or onlines data collection methods in a mere 120 pages is neither realistic nor our goal, does not mean that this book will not enable you to *attain reasonable solutions to difficult problems.* In addition, *you will be able to use templates presented here, modifying them to address your specific your challenges*, and have some fun in the process.

A short book like the one before you cannot do much beyond whetting your appetite, though it goes give enough insight to start making a difference in your job with your new found understanding and passion for social media monitoring, marketing, and auditing.

Tune in to this book's Twitter (@ComMetrics and @WhitePapers) and Google+ (https://plus.google.com/103400392486480765286) accounts for extended examples, illustrations, and pertinent research findings. Of course, our blog (http://ComMetrics.com) and our benchmarking tool (http://My.ComMetrics.com) will also help you stay abreast of the latest tools, trends, and measures.

1.4   Why We Focus on Small- and Medium-Sized Businesses

I am not sure if *you like chips as much as I do,* but in Switzerland, one brand dominates, with about 70% market share - Zweifel Chips. Interestingly, the firm has less than 400 employees, making it a perfect example of how even *smaller companies can gain a dominant position in their respective markets.*

Another important factor is that *99% of all companies in the EU have 250 or fewer employees*, and *96% of all companies in the US have 100 employees or less* putting them in the category of Small- and Medium-Sized business (SME) (Gattiker, Urs E. January 23, 2008—updated August 23, 2011). This illustrates *how important small businesses are to our economy, and how much context matters*: *a small company will not have the budget to copy a large organization's strategy*, will it? No would a business to consumer (B2C) firm use the same strategy to woo clients as a business to business (B2B) company. Finally, non-governmental organizations (NGOs), charities, and government agencies obviously do things a bit differently than for-profit firms do.

Thus, while issues, templates, and methods suggested for completing a comprehensive cost–benefit analysis are of interest to all companies, including global brands, the *main thrust focuses on how these things make sense in the smaller business, NGO or charity context.*

A recent survey of about 400 Swiss companies found that almost 20% have at least one employee dedicated to social media. This is in contrast to global brands that might have hundreds of employees focusing on this area. For instance, in February 2012, *Proctor and Gamble decided to lay off 1,600 staffers, including marketers, as part of its cost cutting* (Gattiker, Urs E. February 7, 2012). At the same time, the company wanted to continue using social media more effectively, as illustrated by its Old Spice campaign (Gattiker, Urs E. September 22, 2011). Regardless of whether these things work out, *costs have to be assessed and compared to the potential benefits of such campaigns. Efforts must also be audited to ensure the ends justify the means.*

I thought this was as good a reason as any to *dedicate this book to the over 95% of companies* that provide the most innovation, creativity, and employment opportunities and pay a sizeable chunk of a country's taxes.

Whenever I explain issues or give another example or case study to illustrate my point, I always keep in mind companies that employ no more than 10, 100, or 400 people. Is this a sensible approach for that type of business or does it apply primarily to the Fortune 500 crowd?

Remember, small businesses—those employing up to 500 people—account for *99% of US businesses, two-thirds of private-sector employment, and half its economic output* (Gattiker, Urs E. January 23, 2008—updated August 23, 2011).

1.5   Where To Start

Generally, we all agree that determining exactly what you wish to accomplish with social media (objectives, goals, dreams, etc.) is essential.

(a) What is *the purpose* of social media for your company?
(b) What is social media's *value proposition*?
(c) What *results* must be achieved with social media and *in what context*?
(d) How will you know when you got there—*measuring and benchmarking*?

Most important in all this is the purpose. Before anybody starts a diet, they have likely determined the purpose of doing so, namely losing weight. If this is the case, we set a time limit and the amount of weight to lose in that time period. We may also want to change food intake (type and amount) to help cut down on salt and sugar consumption.

Similar to a diet, we need to figure out *what purpose we want to use social media and its various tools for.* And while social media is not generally intended to sell products directly, the purpose of its use will be linked to better *serving your customers and/or increasing customer engagement* (Gattiker, Urs E. December 4, 2011).

Table 1.1 Engagement and social media: What is your primary purpose?

Channel's primary purpose	Description by ComMetrics.com	Asking questions
Marketing and sales funnel	The focus is on converting interactions into sales, such as how many people took advantage of the discount offered through Twitter or Facebook	Do early morning posts elicit more responses on your channel than those published at other times?
Customer support	Getting the customer's issue resolved is the primary task, including getting feedback for improving product quality and service	Are clients' issues resolved, even during public holidays or weekends? How does this affect customer satisfaction, repeat purchases?
Social Customer Relationship Management (sCRM) and potential clients	Interacting with clients—feedback, learning to help improve product, and customer experience	Are 20-year-olds potential customers for your Ferrari or power plant? Yes/No but… helps potential clients?
Supplier community	Interacting with suppliers, exchanging ideas and discussing supply chain issues including outsourcing vs. insourcing	Do we need to do this with suppliers, since we are the client? How can we benefit from this?
Just for fun	Trying to stay relevant with the customer, reaching a large number, getting resonance	Where is the potential for your product (B2B vs. B2C)?

Note: This table groups together some major community or blog types to better illustrate the engagement and focus approach (for more information, contact the author)

It is critical that the primary focus is agreed upon, so that content serves this purpose at least 60% of the time. Also, users are not necessarily clients and may never be willing to purchase your product or contribute to your cause (e.g., paying for research to fight a rare disease)

The difficulty is showing how a 9% increase in Secret deodorant sales can be attributed to customer engagement (Gattiker, Urs E. February 7, 2012).

Table 1.1 outlines some of the aims a company or non-profit agency may want to pursue using social media. As with a diet, starting without a goal in mind makes little sense.

Of course, we can probably agree that using social media as a *marketing and sales funnel,* for *customer support, Social Customer Relationship Management* (sCRM) and *potential clients, supplier community,* and *just for fun* each require different actions and content (see Table 1.1).

To illustrate, for an e-commerce site, the social web may primarily be a marketing and sales funnel, while the company selling power plants is unlikely to achieve a sale of a multibillion dollar power plant via the social web. Hence, in the latter scenario, the company will probably focus on reaching out to its potential and current clients to engage and stay in contact.

Nevertheless, in most cases, using social media will not be limited to one category as listed in Table 1.1. In fact, social media use is likely to span across several of these channels. For instance, today's clients will expect some fun and entertainment, even if they joined a discussion group on a social community. An example might be a group on LinkedIn or a community managed by the company on its own servers. In both cases, some fun or a birthday greeting is acceptable. This is even the case if the group were to primarily focus on industry-related matters, such as regulatory changes.

Most channels I come across have something to do with customer support, even something as simple as a client asking where to go for assistance. Of course, this is best accomplished by the client submiting an email form, eliciting a thoughtful response that can also be published on the company's website or in a blog post as an FAQ (frequently asked question). This helps others who may have the same problem find the solution fast, without having to call the customer service hotline.

Social media also helps improve customer relationship management, as repeatedly demonstrated by many examples. Accordingly, while your organization may focus on a particular type of social media use such as sCRM, a Twitter account may do more, including distributing interesting information to suppliers and/or potential clients (Twitter is rarely ever the best way to help your clients get their problem resolved—Gattiker, Urs E. February 12, 2012).

1.6 The Maturity Model

The maturity model in Table 1.2 outlines and articulates your organization's technology use as a four-stage model, whereby the organization begins as a novice, moves on to early adopter, then to evangelist, adopter, and finally optimizer.

Accordingly, as a *novice*, the organization may still be a newcomer to this technology or Web 2.0, in contrast to some of your employees, who may already have been using various social media tools and technologies for quite some time. For instance, photo sharing through Flickr or Picasa could be popular among your staff, as well as having an account on Facebook or Pinterest. As an *early adopter*, the company may still be exploring ways to use technology better, such as Twitter, blogs, or Facebook. The focus is still on budget and direct costs. The *evangelist* is further ahead and tries to develop actionable metrics to benchmark and see how things influence key drivers (e.g., customer satisfaction). Some indirect costs are monitored, while most direct costs are known and accounted for.

The *adopter stage* involves acceptance and widespread use of the technology. It means the company is trying to foster more engagement with its target audience, such as potential customers and current clients. Most indirect costs are assessed and some benefits materializing from these efforts have been identified. Of course, understanding how these may explain increased sales can be rather difficult, as in the example of Procter & Gamble (P&G) on Facebook (Gattiker, Urs E. February 12, 2012).

The *optimizer* type of organization manages its indirect and direct costs using full cost accounting. The effects on key drivers are understood and monitored, while opportunity costs have also been identified.

Table 1.2 Maturity model for social media

State	Description by ComMetrics.com	Cost–benefit analysis
Novice—discovery *phase 1*	A few people participate and discover new tools, identifying consumer tech gadgets that could impact the business Some staff may already use various tools privately (e.g., Skype, Facebook, Gmail, Flickr, Pinterest)	–Few tools used –Limited cost data
Early adopter— exploration *phase 2*	A few more people experiment and test tools, approaches, methods, etc., with the intention of rapid quick failure in order to learn and improve quickly Exploring ways to measure goal attainment	–Budget for social media –Focus is on tracking certain direct costs
Evangelist— practice, trial and connection *phase 3*	Managers open to change and new technology seek repeatable processes and support pilot projects with the new technology, tools, platforms, etc. Developing actionable metrics for benchmarking	–Some indirect costs are identified and monitored –Most direct costs are known and accounted for (e.g., materials, labor, and expenses)
Adopter— acceptance and focus on engagement *phase 4*	Successful pilot projects and/or evangelization lead to increased use across the enterprise. Processes become repeatable and predictable, and are now managed Identifying and applying social business metrics that relate to and influence key drivers (e.g., product returns, repeat sales)	–Indirect costs (e.g., materials, labor, and expenses) are monitored –Some social media marketing or social business benefits are quantified and tracked
Optimizer— cooperation and facilitation *phase 5*	Processes are improved and the company expands adoption throughout its ecosystem in order to better serve stakeholders (e.g., channel partners) Focus is on customer centricity for better revenue growth Online accountability—moving from hindsight to insight	–Full cost accounting –The effects of social media on key drivers (e.g., customer complaints) are regularly measured and monitored –Opportunity costs are identified and well understood

Note: Employees may use a variety of tools (e.g., LinkedIn) privately. While the organization may be an adopter when it comes to its website or blog, it may be an evangelist with Facebook and/or novice with Twitter, for example

Clearly, the further along the organization is with regard to technology adoption, the better it may understand the challenges and opportunities social media offers. Therefore, a company in the adopter stage (phase 4) will likely do an extensive cost–benefit analysis of its social media activities (see Chapter 2), and regularly use its audit data to increase its performance improvement, when compared to a novice (phase 1).

Finally, as the note in Table 1.2 points out, an organization may be a novice with regard to its blog and website usage, while having gained considerable experience with its Facebook page. What is important to remember is that *just because more resources, including labor, were spent on one technology, does not necessarily mean it is more advantageous than any other*. Regardless of what stage the company might be positioned at when it comes to social media, it must harness internal know-how and resources, since its employees may be further along in the maturity model.

As they pertain to cost-benefit analysis, these issues are outlined in more detail in the next chapter.

1.7   How We Organized This Book

This book provides some templates and checklists that are part of the CyTRAP Social Media Audit Toolkit (*CySoMAT*) of which we use a more extensive and detailed version to audit our clients' social media marketing activities, as well as our own.

Figure 1.1 illustrates this in the form of a pyramid where Chapter 1 (you are here) provides an introduction to the topic, how we intend to approach it, and walk you through some of our tools.

Chapter 2 focuses on investigating the direct and indirect costs of social media activities, including but not limited to establishing, maintaining, and engaging with clients through Facebook or Google+. In both cases, we need to have some discussions about the direct and indirect costs involved that might make the project more or less feasible. Without this understanding, it is difficult to audit and assess performance of activities and benchmark them against our objectives.

Chapter 3 offers some insight regarding what one should be doing before the actual audit happens. This work *applies regardless if this is an internal audit or one conducted by an external party*. Before the audit starts, certain documentation needs to be prepared. By doing so, some of the most obvious shortcomings may be discovered and can hopefully be addressed before the actual audit begins.

Chapter 4 continues in this realm and outlines issues regarding the focus and scope of the audit. For instance, an audit may focus on your Facebook page, Twitter account, and blog or just one of the three. The scope may include an in-depth analysis involving all the steps of the audit as outlined in templates from Chapters 5

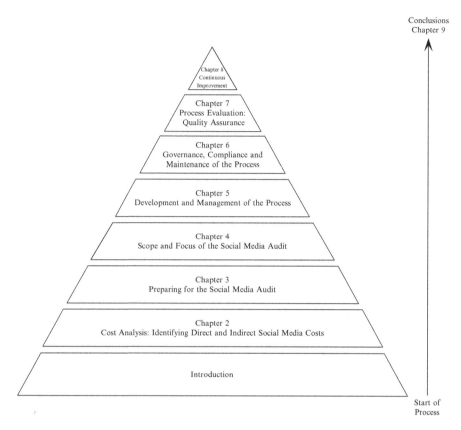

Conclusions
Chapter 9

Start of
Process

Fig. 1.1 Managing the social media audit building blocks of the CyTRAP Social Media Audit Toolkit (CySoMAT). The model represents a process cycle whereby the conclusion or wrap-up is the beginning of a new audit cycle (back to start)

through 9 or, only a portion thereof. The chapter also presents the scoring system we use in the CyTRAP Social Media Audit Toolkit (CySoMAT).

Chapter 5 discusses how we can audit the management of a process, such as developing the Google+ page a Facebook page, posting content on the corporate blog, or other social media activities.

Chapter 6 addresses the important issue of governance and maintenance of the process, including compliance matters that require resolution. This includes matters of document archiving and producing the necessary digital files in case of e-discovery.

As Figure 1.1 illustrates, Chapter 7 tries to shed some light on the process evaluation and *quality assurance* of the organization's social media activities. Quality assurance is a particular concern to ensure the brand's image is not tarnished in any way or form by different social media activities in different country divisions and so forth.

Chapter 8 then focuses on improvement. Accordingly, data collected during the audit as described above must first be analyzed. Based on insights gained in this process, areas of improvement must be identified. Furthermore, objectives will have to be set that determine when what kinds of improvements must be achieved.

Chapter 9, the conclusion, marks the wrap-up. It is best to understand Figure 1.1 as a cycle that once completed, begins again. Audits and evaluations are needed on a regular basis to make sure that performance targets are met and social media marketing activities are up to par.

1.8 Using the Audit Process to Make Better Choices

The CyTRAP Social Media Audit Toolkit (CySoMAT) helps organizations and decision makers replace their intuition with formal analysis. This enables taking into account data on all known variables, while being able to quantify all available choices. This method has been shown to significantly improve decisions in contexts like school admissions and hiring (Milkman, Chugh, & Bazerman, 2009). Of course, considering multiple options simultaneously rather than separately can optimize outcomes. It also increases the team's will power in carrying out a choice made for social media activities.

Moreover, the CySoMAT encourages a *team approach*. Hence, we focus on decision making by committee rather than individually since this *can improve decisions in group contexts*. By documenting the information used in this decision-making process, *individuals can be made accountable for their choices* (Milkman, Chugh, & Bazerman, 2009).

As suggested by research (e.g., Wargo 2007), people tend to get overwhelmed with facts and data, which may cause them to overestimate a certain risk at first. Hence, facts uncovered with the help of the CySoMAT need to be communicated in such a way as, "We are at some risk of being noncompliant according to regulation XYZ and we should check in order to make any necessary changes quickly." Such an approach may be a more powerful motivator for making better decisions than just the raw score. And when statistics are presented regarding audit findings, doing so in easy-to-grasp graphic format instead of numerically can help stakeholders (as well as auditors, who can be as statistically challenged as most laypeople) gain their own insights from the facts (Wargo 2007).

1.9 Summary and Conclusion

This chapter outlined who should read this book and who should refrain from doing so. In addition, Table 1.1 enumerates the different purposes one might have for using social media. As pointed out in the text, it is likely that a company uses a combination thereof. Needless to say, whatever is decided, the purpose needs to be spelled out succinctly in order to develop a clear and straightforward strategy.

Table 1.2 presented the maturity model for social media and the five phases that characterize an organization's situation when it comes to social media usage. The further along the organization is on this continuum, the more likely it will have a better understanding of the costs and benefits entailed with using social media. As well, the company's goals and metrics will be more developed in phase 5 than one would normally expect in phase 3 or most certainly phase 2.

Figure 1.1 provides the reader with an overall view of how this book's chapters fit together and can be used in one's own work setting.

The next chapter will provide an introduction to cost–benefit analysis and provide a framework for analyzing a company's Facebook page.

References

Gattiker, Urs E. (January 23, 2008—updated August 23, 2011). European Commission: Defining the term SME. [Blog post - ComMetrics]. Retrieved August 23, 2011, from http://commetrics. com/?p=16

Gattiker, Urs, E. (September 22, 2011). Going viral or selling product: ROI anyone? [Blog post - ComMetrics]. Retrieved February 6, 2012, from http://commetrics.com/?p=16696/

Gattiker, Urs E. (December 4, 2011). ComMetrics 2012 social media trends: Engagement. [Blog post - ComMetrics]. Retrieved December 15, 2011, from http://commetrics.com/?p=17331

Gattiker, Urs E. (February 5, 2012). Facebook: why is nobody listening? [Blog post - ComMetrics]. Retrieved February6, 2012, from http://commetrics.com/?p=18203/

Gattiker, Urs E. (February 7, 2012). Facebook: why is nobody listening?—P&G and Secret's 9 percent sales increase [Blog comment - ComMetrics]. Retrieved February 6, 2012, from http:// commetrics.com/?p=18203/

Gattiker, Urs E. (February 12, 2012). Social CRM: Kundenservice mit Twitter? [Blog post - CyTRAP]. Retrieved March 27, 2012, from http://info.cytrap.eu/?p=3122/

Milkman KL, Chugh D, Bazerman MH (2009). How can decision making be improved? Perspectives on Psychological Science 4, 379–383

Wargo E (2007). More than just the facts: helping patients make informed choices. Cornell University, Department of Human Development: Outreach and Extension. Retrieved February 6, 2012, from http://www.human.cornell.edu/hd/outreach-extension/loader.cfm?csModule=security/ getfiles&PageID=43508

Chapter 2
Cost Analysis: Identifying Direct and Indirect Social Media Costs

Abstract Managers want a good idea about costs, both direct and indirect. Most important are follow-up expenses or those incurred once the equipment or web domain has been purchased. This chapter focuses on these issues and outlines in straightforward language how your company can get a better handle on costs incurred for such things as a Facebook page, Twitter account, or corporate blog.

My first serious use of cost-benefit analysis was in trying to address how young people entering the workforce in the province of Alberta (Canada) might best be helped by government programs that facilitate skills upgrading. The focus was on whether more general skills (i.e., those skills that can be transferred to another job) versus specific skills (e.g., specific to one's occupation) would help improve job prospects for trainees. This issue has been addressed extensively in the literature, including human capital theory as proposed by Gary Becker (1964). Other applications include helping organizations determine which recruiting or selection method facilitated hiring qualified staff using a cost–benefit framework.

The objective of cost–benefit analysis is to determine the change in net benefits brought about by a new or amended marketing activity, *in our case social media*. The cost–benefit analysis should be carried out in an incremental manner. That is, the incremental benefits and costs of each of the alternative options are estimated and compared to the baseline option.

It is obvious that understanding exactly what you want to measure and how to measure it takes time. Accordingly, you cannot expect to have this completely nailed down before you begin. Nevertheless, cost–benefit analysis will be an important exercise to help you use social media more effectively.

Cost–benefit analysis *helps managers get clear and accessible information on the economic pros and cons associated with social media and marketing* investments, so that they *can identify the activities that are both effective and affordable for their organization*. This permits a better allocation of scarce resources.

U.E. Gattiker, *Social Media Audit: Measure for Impact*, SpringerBriefs
in Computer Science, DOI 10.1007/978-1-4614-3603-4_2, © The Author(s) 2013

In this chapter we focus on costs. When starting a social media activity and depending on where you are on the maturity continuum (see Table 1.2), cost information may be more or less extensive. In most cases, quantifying the benefits is much harder, and goes beyond the scope of this chapter. Nevertheless, we can point out that *with the help of actionable metrics that link to key drivers*, the importance of social media can be demonstrated. To illustrate, using Twitter may help reduce wait times for walk-in traffic at our restaurant during lunch, specifically by tweeting a code to our followers that offers regulars who place their order before 11:30 am or after 1:30 pm a free soft drink. The code can then be used track how much this action helps reduce patrons' wait to be seated and receive their order, a key driver that affects turnover.

Using Facebook and/or the organization's Google+ page as an example, we outline step by step how potential costs and benefits can be assessed systematically. While our framework is far from complete, it does give the reader an idea of what needs to be done to better present a case to top management. It begins with assessing things before deciding to establish a page, as well as setting it up and monitoring its progress while being able to show the budget committee the numbers.

2.1   Planning to Set Up a Facebook or Google+ Page

Table 2.1 outlines the strategic costs one should consider when thinking about setting up and running a Facebook fanpage.

You may not want to set a precise budget (material, labor, expenses/overhead separated into direct and indirect costs) right away. Nevertheless, your budget committee will want to see numbers in order to approve your funding request. Accordingly, streamlining this process is a must. Table 2.1 will help you achieve this objective by outlining the types of issues that must be addressed before launching a Facebook or Google+ page.

To support your efforts, expenditures must be grouped into *indirect costs* (also *known collectively as overhead—cannot be attributed directly to a product, service, or department*) and *direct costs*. Each cost type can be attributed to one of three categories:

- Materials
- Labor
- Expenses or overhead

However, to do this properly, we must specify the two or three critical tasks we want visitors to perform during their visit. To illustrate, a firm that offers consumers local searches if they need to find a dentist or bookstore may want visitors to conduct a search directly from its Facebook page. By contrast, an engineering firm might want visitors to download their eBook that helps people prepare a tender, or another teaser that provides value to the interested Google+ follower.

This indicates that *we must identify and agree on what critical tasks we want visitors to perform*. Thereafter, we need to set measurable objectives and our progress must be tracked over time to see if the trend is going in the right direction (e.g., increasing monthly active users and number of comments for each post).

Table 2.1 What Facebook really costs you: Planning

Description by ComMetrics.com	Direct costs	Indirect costs
Determine your target audience (e.g., age group, country, gender, and education)— may require research, outside consultant, etc.	Labor, material, expense	–
Establish the three most important goals a Facebook brand page should help you accomplish (*engagement*, visibility—be specific!)	Labor	–
Ascertain the three most important tasks clients need to complete during their visit (e.g., Like a post, comment, and shop)	Expense or overhead	–
Plan how your Facebook page can best be integrated with your Web site and/or corporate blog (i.e., coordination of strategy and content to be shared/published)	Labor, material, expense	Material
Develop three key performance indicators (KPIs) to help measure progress over the next quarter	Labor	Expense
Coordinate next quarter's Facebook activities with other channels (e.g., exhibitions, advertising, and PR)	Labor	Labor
Set a social media policy and discuss other legal matters, such as liability and compliance issues	Labor	Expense
Design your Facebook page	Expense	–
Train staff and hold workshops (in-house or through outside experts)	Labor, expense	–
Strategize for a worst-case scenario within your crisis management framework (e.g., how employees should respond to negative comments about the company and products on the Facebook page)	Labor, expense	–
Opportunity costs: Determine whether the time and money spent on Facebook might be used more effectively on other platforms (e.g., LinkedIn, Tencent Weibo, Xing, corporate blog)	Labor, material, expense	Labor, material, expense

Note. This table groups together some major cost items to better illustrate the full cost accounting approach (for more information, contact the author). Thanks to Susanne Ulrich for improvements made to an earlier version of this table

It is also necessary to make sure that we plan how Facebook activities will be integrated with other activities. For instance, should the Facebook fanpage URL be added to our stationary as with our corporate Web site and blog? Will we publish a link on our Facebook page for every new blog post? Or will we start a discussion by writing a note on Facebook instead?

Table 2.2 What Facebook really costs you: Implementation

Description by ComMetrics.com	Direct costs	Indirect costs
Engage PR to create a press release for the new fanpage (using social media and other distribution channels)	Labor, expense	–
Prepare editorial calendar for posts	Labor	–
Set up assistance from in-house experts	Labor, expense	–
Set up assistance from outside experts	Expense	Material
Integrate with corporate blog/Web site (e.g., Like button on blog posts)	Labor	–
Create apps for better customer engagement (e.g., online polls for fans and easy-to-use contact form)	Expense or overhead	–
Marketing campaign to connect with clients and target audience (e.g., Facebook, corporate blog, and Twitter)	Expense	Expense
Vanity URL for Facebook page	–	Expense
Opportunity costs: Determine whether the time and money spent on Facebook might be used more effectively on other platforms (e.g., LinkedIn, Tencent Weibo, Xing, corporate blog)	Labor, material, expense	Labor, material, expense

Note: This table groups together some major cost items to better illustrate the full cost accounting approach (for more information, contact the author). Thanks to Susanne Ulrich for improvements made to an earlier version of this table

The above issues must be discussed, especially since they have consequences for the costs we will incur. Of course, it is less time consuming to ensure that a tweet on Twitter is simultaneously posted on the company's Facebook page. Nevertheless, this approach is less likely to foster engagement through comments and a discussion by fans than a note specifically tailored to Facebook users, with just a link to the blog.

Table 2.1 demonstrates that it never hurts to compare the effort and resources spent on social media like Facebook to what it would take to prepare for a trade show, an ad in a newspaper, and/or publish another corporate magazine. Enumerating any and all potential opportunity costs is practical and therefore very helpful.

The table also provides a list of several issues and questions that should be addressed during the planning period. Once strategic and planning issues have been addressed, including costs and budget issues as outlined in Table 2.1, implementation matters come to the fore. Table 2.2 tries to structure these issues in some more detail.

2.2 Implementing a Facebook or Google+ Page

Focusing direct and indirect costs is required as part of implementation matters, using the categories listed in Table 2.2. Some costs are so immaterial or negligible that it is not feasible to track them, even if they are fully traceable. In this case, we may just enter expenses/overhead under indirect costs.

Depending on where your company resides within the social business maturity model (see Table 1.2), costs will be more or less easily traceable. Accordingly, if this is your tenth fanpage for just another of the company's brands, it will be a little easier: you will have learned from past mistakes and be able to more accurately estimate project numbers. Of course, this assumes that knowledge is shared across divisions and brands, which unfortunately is not always the case.

In some cases, you might also be able to piggyback with, and benefit from, another project, such as using a Facebook URL to promote a product or event. The URL might already be known by your target audience since it is already listed on stationary and print ads. Such piggybacking might justify charging indirect costs—overhead to the project for use of a well-known URL or account.

Distilling direct and indirect costs can be somewhat tricky early on in the social business maturity model. Nevertheless, keeping track of these costs, including the work time spent in making it happen, is a must to be able to show how this could benefit operations.

Using Twitter or Tencent Weibo may also be a must for some companies, but for many—including non-profits—it may not be financially viable or strategically smart to use all of these platforms. To illustrate, the Facebook platform may not be the best way to find those who might purchase your high-speed trains, power plants, or architectural services. Let us not forget that a recent study reported that for US consumers, Facebook is primarily a channel to get news from friends and family (Mitchell et al. March, 2012).

2.3   Maintaining Your Facebook or Google+ Presence

As you can see in the above title, I have added the word Google+ because any page or group you intend to set up will incur costs, no matter what the platform. Accordingly, benefits that can or did accrue must be spelled out for the benefit of the budget committee, enabling you to make a decision that will most likely give you the results you seek.

After we have planned and implemented the Facebook page for one of our brands, it is necessary to manage the interaction. In Table 2.3, we outline some of the costs to consider when managing the interaction needed to maintain the fanpage's attractiveness for those who Like it. As Feile (February 28, 2011) pointed out, some of the tasks to consider for a hotel could include putting up guest comments, or getting them to post their feedback and photos from their last stay on your Wall. Of course, the hotel might put up some event videos, as well as job vacancies, and so forth. Whatever is shared (e.g., images or customer comments) must be vetted to protect clients' privacy (e.g., removing names on customer comments). This is especially important in cases where faces in images can be tagged on Facebook or Google+.

A firm that offers consumers local searches for services and stores may want visitors to conduct a search directly from its Facebook page. Therefore, *when*

Table 2.3 What Facebook really costs you: Interaction

Description by ComMetrics.com	Direct costs	Indirect costs
Gathering information on the Web to post content valued by fans (i.e., more than company news)	Labor	Labor, expense
Selecting and preparing content for release (e.g., a Wall post or a Note with video)	Labor	
Writing one piece of content every week (e.g., explaining something of interest and asking questions to engage fans)	Labor	
Rephrasing and cross posting replies to comments made on the corporate blog to elicit feedback	Labor	
Acknowledging and responding to fan-engagement (e.g., a post Like or Wall comment)	Labor	
Opportunity costs: Determine whether the time and money spent on Facebook might be used more effectively on other platforms (e.g., LinkedIn, Tencent Weibo, Xing, corporate blog)	Labor, material, expense	Labor, material, expense

Note: This table groups together some major cost items to better illustrate the full cost accounting approach (for more information, contact the author). Thanks to Susanne Ulrich for improvements made to an earlier version of this table

maintaining and updating the Facebook page, content has to relate to the primary product. For an engineering firm, this could mean a new ISO standard or regulation that will affect its clients' businesses.

As such, engaging content does not mean retweeting a Twitter post on your Wall. While this saves time, it is unlikely to elicit much engagement from Facebook users.

2.4 Perform Maintenance Tasks Early in the Day

Remember that about 15% of employers block Facebook access, so new content must be posted early in the morning—preferably before 7:00 A.M.—to catch smartphone users on their daily commute. Research shows that people are more likely to leave a comment or Like something if things are posted earlier in the day.

As previously stated, it never hurts to compare the effort and resources spent on social media to the resources required for an alternative media activity - awareness of all potential costs is essential.

Table 2.4 focuses on things people tend to forget. For instance, Facebook changes from time to time, so staff may require a refresher seminar to acquire new skills (e.g., correct privacy settings to disable geo-tagging). Also, besides having a crisis communication procedure in place, people need to learn how to effectively handle any negative onslaught—even on weekends (Nestlé did not do so well when Greenpeace attacked).

Table 2.4   What Facebook really costs you: Maintenance

Description by ComMetrics.com	Direct costs	Indirect costs
Coordinating Facebook activities with other social media campaigns, PR, etc.	–	Expense or overhead
In-house and outside training to update skills	Labor, expense	
Facebook project manager's wages	–	Labor
Programming new and maintaining existing Facebook apps to improve fans' experience	Labor, expense	
Applications used to manage Facebook more effectively (e.g., conducting polls and contact forms)	Expense or overhead	
Conducting fire drills: ensuring strategies developed for worst-case scenarios within your crisis management plan work in practice by testing them out (e.g., how employees should respond to negative comments about the company and products on the Facebook page)	Labor	Expense
Learning from negative feedback to improve your product(s)—regular discussions with engineering and sales	–	Labor, expense
Mobile Internet access to manage Facebook on the weekend and during your commute	–	Expense or overhead
Opportunity costs: Determine whether the time and money spent on Facebook might be used more effectively on other platforms (e.g., LinkedIn, Tencent Weibo, Xing, corporate blog)	Labor, material, expense	Labor, material, expense

Note: This table groups together some major cost items to better illustrate the full cost accounting approach (for more information, contact the author). Thanks to Susanne Ulrich for improvements made to an earlier version of this table

Learning from negative feedback is critical, but necessary procedures must be in place to take advantage of such information (see Table 2.1).

Another example is using polls to elicit feedback, while giving fans the chance to share their assessment of certain issues. Such feedback is rapid and invaluable, even though responding to it properly takes some time—crowdsourcing at its best.

Finally, it is *not always clear whether costs are direct or indirect*. For instance, if people already have mobile Internet to answer e-mail, it might not make sense to charge direct costs for people using the service to work on the company's fanpage, but noting an overhead charge might suffice.

Each company must decide such issues for itself to ensure the effort made to assign costs is not higher than the expense or material spent. Nevertheless, depending on where your company resides within the social business maturity model (see Table 1.2), costs will be more or less easily traceable (i.e., the higher up in the model you are, the easier it will be to trace).

2.5 Running a Promotion

Lots of people suggest that some advertising is needed to promote your Facebook page.

Transforming a Facebook fan into a customer takes hard work. Facebook's own guidelines dictate that anyone running a sweepstakes on their Facebook page must get written approval from a Facebook account representative. In order to get one of those, you have to spend about US$10,000 on advertising with the company. Some have suggested that Facebook has eased up on these rules, but as long as they remain listed, one should probably abide by them to avoid trouble.

Remember that setting performance objectives is critical for the campaign, and metrics must be developed and agreed upon as outlined in our blog post, Measuring Facebook engagement: What is good? (published March 14, 2011). Accordingly, if you have less than 10,000 fans (individuals that clicked Like), increasing engagement from about 0.6% to 1.2% could be considered a success. However, depending on which study you look at and how engagement is measured (e.g., clicking the Like button is passive engagement, writing a comment takes more effort), studies suggest an average of less than 0.4% of readers or fans engage with your comment. Of course, free product will change this. Whether those fans who are attracted by that free product will stick around after the sweepstakes is another question. Most important, are they the type of clients you as a tool and die maker, consultant, or coffee shop are after?

2.6 Account for All Campaign Costs

In Table 2.6, we outline the costs of handing out these deals or product samples. For instance, content to give away, such as eBooks, must be created and readied for distribution. Running a Facebook campaign also requires an advertising budget, as well as product to give away. Moreover, a discount voucher may reduce your profit margin and, most importantly, nobody likes to give discounts to clients that would have made a purchase regardless.

Remember the "Buy 2, get the 3rd FREE" promotion? Even though we might not need that many of whatever is for sale, we still buy them because people always love specials. But this also means lost revenue and any other costs incurred by the campaign must be assessed, as outlined in Table 2.6.

2.7 What About Pinterest, Twitter, Second Life, and Others?

Most questions listed in Tables 2.1, 2.2, 2.3, 2.4, 2.5, and 2.6 can be used to assess the cost of being active on many different platforms by simply replacing Facebook as a word in the sentence. However, for small companies, this is not much of an

Table 2.5   What Facebook really costs you: Promotions

Description by ComMetrics.com	Direct costs	Indirect costs
Brainstorming and planning a new campaign (e.g., discount coupon)	–	Expense or overhead
Setting objectives for improvement in engagement levels as a result of the campaign (Like(s), comments, uploaded of user content, etc.) and monitoring these engagement metrics (e.g., post engagement or reach rate, post interaction, and unsubscribe rate)	Labor, material, expense	–
Designing the campaign (e.g., special discount for people who Like the page)	Labor, expense	–
Preparing texts and layouts for the campaign/ sweepstakes	Labor, expense	–
Planning and organizing a sweepstakes that requires some action for participants to qualify	Labor, material, expense	–
Obtaining legal approval for the campaign/ sweepstakes	Expense	–
Time spent monitoring the campaign and responding to requests by fans	Labor	–
Monitoring participants' level of engagement 60–90 days after the campaign's end (fighting the give-me-the-freebie-now-so-I-can-disappear-until-the-next-campaign syndrome)	Expense or overhead	–
Measuring and monitoring the campaign's new user generation (i.e., clicking Like to participate), vs. engaging paying customers (those who regularly purchase your product)	Labor, material, expense	–
Opportunity costs: Determine whether the time and money spent on Facebook might be used more effectively on other platforms (e.g., LinkedIn, Tencent Weibo, Xing, corporate blog)	Labor, material, expense	Labor, material, expense

Note: This table groups together some major cost items to better illustrate the full cost accounting approach (for more information, contact the author). Thanks to Susanne Ulrich for improvements made to an earlier version of this table

issue. For starters, it is highly unlikely that it has the resources to be active on several platforms, and you must first ensure your clients are already active on whatever platforms you may be considering. If you manufacture screws or build boats, your clients may not want to connect with you on Facebook, but they might be willing to view pictures on Flickr or Pinterest. They might even be interested in reading your blog, which includes additional unique content, such as a 2-minute video. Of course, they might also want to listen to a short podcast downloaded from iTunes.

There is no way to participate everywhere but, we should never forget that our central hub should be our blog and/or Web site. In turn, our Facebook activities or YouTube videos must always link back to our hub, where people can find more interesting information, such as checklists and/or white papers, blog posts, and so

Table 2.6 What Facebook really costs you: Exclusive deals and discounts

Description	Direct costs	Indirect costs
Deciding how special or unique content will be created and by whom (e.g., eBooks, checklists, coupons, and discount codes)		Expense or overhead
Producing content using internal know-how or outside experts (e.g., eBook: How to write a successful tender for a government contract)	Labor, expense	Labor, expense
Creating an eBook, checklist for free download and/or research report (e.g., company could hire a polling firm to do a survey)	Labor	Expense
Actual costs of providing fans with a product sample or discount coupon (e.g., additional sales minus discount)	Expense	
Measuring converted winner coupons (how many issued, vs. how many redeemed)	Labor, expense	
Cost of buying a prize if you cannot provide it from your own products (e.g., a search engine cannot issue coupons like a pizza restaurant can) and/or time spent finding a partner	Labor, expense	
Lost profits—a discount may nullify profits for that sales transaction. Some might have purchased your product anyway, but thanks to the discount, they pay a price that lowers your overall profit margin	Expense	
Opportunity costs: Determine whether the time and money spent on Facebook might be used more effectively on other platforms (e.g., LinkedIn, Tencent Weibo, Xing, corporate blog)	Labor, material, expense	Labor, material, expense

Note: This table groups together some major cost items to better illustrate the full cost accounting approach (for more information, contact the author). Thanks to Susanne Ulrich for improvements made to an earlier version of this table

forth. For this reason, content can be posted elsewhere, but it should link back to your social media hub (e.g., Web site or blog) to help improve your search result performance. In other words, search engines have an easier time finding relevant content on your blog than on Facebook, Twitter, or Google+.

2.8   Twitter and Social Customer Relationship Management

Lots of companies use Twitter or Facebook as a channel to provide better customer service. What we one challenge here is that most customer service hotline work is outsourced, while social media inquiries are generally handled internally by staff with much more expertise about the company's products than an employee at an outsourcer's will ever have. Internal staff also tend to earn more and be better educated than their outsourced peers.

Unless we are willing to *compare apples to apples* (i.e., engineers handling incoming inquiries, whether via Twitter or the call center) things can neither be easily nor fairly compared. Needless to say, valuing a request for help more highly if it comes via social media (i.e., the person publically asks for help), than if it comes through a call center seems unfair. Your clients certainly will not appreciate that. It also ignores the reality that customers still prefer talking to a human being when resolving complex problems (e.g., fixing my Internet modem or getting my SIM card to work on my mobile).

Whenever we have had a chance to figure out direct and indirect costs regarding client service requests, the in-house call center wins. Not only are the costs about the same as for using social media, but more importantly, the customer gets a solution sooner, and will likely tell others about what a positive experience they had (*word-of-mouth marketing*). With Twitter, it takes several tweets that may still result in the client having to speak with the customer service hotline to get the matter resolved. Of course, you can tell the Twitter user to follow you so you can follow them back. Then, they can send you a direct message with their phone number so your competent agent can call them to solve the issue. However, this should be the exception and not the rule. Instead, provide the means and level of service for inquiries via e-mail and the customer service hotline that make using Twitter unnecessary (Gattiker, February 12, 2012).

Of course, if you are a FT Global 500 company, you may still have a Twitter account to provide customers with an opportunity to reach out to you if needed. But for a SME, it does not seem the right way to go considering costs and benefits.

2.9 Conclusion

The above templates combine to provide a step-by-step checklist for assessing what your Facebook or Google+ page might cost. In particular, we addressed the issue of direct versus indirect costs.

In case of unknown prices, one could use a shadow price (a price estimate collected from outside the company). For instance, if one does not know how much it will cost to produce website content, *economists sometimes use as an estimate the price that a third party would charge for maintaining a Facebook page*. While this may only be a rough estimate and not include all possible costs, it provides a good idea. But if your internal costs are higher, you had better streamline things to get budget approval.

Without some type of budget, it will be difficult to set performance targets and achieve them. Unless you have some idea of how much time it will take to manage a Google+ page according to the objectives set, you may be seeing in the dark. For instance, the type of content that must be created, curated, posted, as well as at what frequency mean certain basic cost levels are involved to achieve things well. While many companies might agree that 20–40% of their marketing budget is allocated for social media, just having a budget is not enough. You must track your costs to accomplish the things you wish to.

The templates presented in this chapter and the issues addressed there in provide a systematic way to achieve better cost transparency for each of your projects, such as a corporate blog, Facebook, or Google+ page.

In the next chapter, we will begin outlining how a company can prepare itself for a social media audit.

References

Becker, Gary. (1964). Human Capital. New York: National Bureau of Economic Research

Bitkom (Bundesverband Informationswirtschaft, Telekommunikation und neue Medien e.V.) (March 12, 2012). Suchmaschinen sind die beliebtesten Startseiten im Web (Search engines are the most popular start pages for web browsers). [Online press release by Bitkom.de] Retrieved March 31, 2012 from http://www.bitkom.org/de/presse/8477_71475.aspx

Gattiker, Urs E. (February 12, 2012). Social CRM: Kundenservice mit Twitter? (Social CRM: Customer service with Twitter?). [Blog post—info CyTRAP.eu]. Retrieved February 12, 2012 from http://info.cytrap.eu/?p=3122

Mitchell, Amy, Rosenstiel, Tom, and Christian, Leah (March 2012). What Facebook and Twitter mean for news. [Published online: The Pew Research Center's Project for Excellence in Journalism. The State of the News media 2012—An Annual Report on American Journalism) Retrieved March 28, 2012, from http://stateofthemedia.org/2012/mobile-devices-and-news-consumption-some-good-signs-for-journalism/what-facebook-and-twitter-mean-for-news/#fnref-11554-1

Chapter 3
Preparing for the Social Media Audit

Abstract This chapter introduces the CyTRAP Social Media Audit Toolkit (CySoMAT), which helps score and appraise your organization's performance using social media Web 2.0 tools and interacting with the social customer.

In the previous chapter, we addressed cost issues. Templates were provided to assess activities such as establishing and maintaining a corporate blog, or Facebook or Google+ page, and engaging with readers through those channels. Assessing the costs associated with such an endeavor is important during the social media audit, because it provides a better understanding of what it takes to produce content and activities that are valued by your target audience, such as existing and potential clients.

The social media audit is an objective assurance and consulting activity designed to add value and improve an organization's social media operations. A systematic, disciplined approach to evaluating and enhancing the effectiveness of risk management, compliance, and governance helps an organization review and improve its performance.

As stated earlier, the book provides a set of templates and checklists that can be used to systematically assess your organization's social media activities and improve the firm's social media footprint (e.g., ComMetrics Footprint).

In this chapter, I discuss what should be addressed before the actual audit process begins. Accordingly, the scope of the audit and how extensive it needs to be should be agreed upon and spelled out. The forms below are a first step in structuring this work and approaching it systematically.

Unfortunately, Preparing for the social media audit is often perceived as a painful at necessary evil, not so different from some performance appraisals. Everybody knows it is required by management and/or the union, so both the manager and the employee go through the motions. However, when performance appraisals are used effectively, managers know that the employee needs to be prepared well in advance, including offering informal feedback. This will help the employee show improvement in the upcoming appraisal when compared to the last one, while reaching agreed upon objectives.

U.E. Gattiker, *Social Media Audit: Measure for Impact*, SpringerBriefs in Computer Science, DOI 10.1007/978-1-4614-3603-4_3, © The Author(s) 2013

The same principle can be applied when preparing for an internal or external social media audit. For instance, you may want to have everything for an August audit ready by May 1 giving you the month of May to discuss things with your team and already make some adjustments and improvements. That leaves June and July to see how things improve and make slight further adjustments if necessary. Accordingly, when the actual audit (or performance appraisal) occurs in August, the team will be ready and able to show improvements over the last few months.

To illustrate, while preparing for the audit, the team may discover the occurrence of several nonconformities in behavior in the preceding months. For instance, several staff tweeted items that could be seen as violating some people's privacy and/or other rights, such as intellectual property. The unfortunate thing is that the team discovers that these incidents were not documented in any way or recorded systematically. Moreover, these incidents were not discussed with those that possibly violated privacy, copyright, and/or social media guidelines. Worse, these cases were not used to illustrate such nonconformities staff training or skills upgrading. Documenting such cases makes using them to allow staff to learn from such incidents feasible.

Discovering nonconformities while preparing for an audit provides a great opportunity to start improvements right away. Put differently, why wait until the auditor visits and pay to be told that this nonconformity must be addressed when you already knew about it months ago? If while preparing for the audit you find that some things are not as you would like, you can begin improvements before the audit even starts. Doing so not only gets the team psyched up for the audit but, more importantly, fosters continuous improvement that can then also be documented.

What does this mean for the social media audit? As discussed above, We must schedule the audit and related changes around certain dates (e.g., August).

3.1 Things To Keep in Mind

For the sake of simplicity, we refer in the following checklist and review documents primarily to such services as Twitter, Facebook, Quora, LinkedIn, Viadeo, Xing, corporate blogs, Pinterest (the latest darling https://plus.google.com/b/ 1034003924 86480765286/103400392486480765286/posts/bgtphkJKvUG), and so forth.

During your audit, you can replace and add whatever service seems most relevant in the context of your company's social media activities.

For any audit, context matters a great deal, including:

- Type of organization (e.g., NGO, charity vs. public listed company)
- Size of company
- Type of product (consumer vs. capital goods or services)
- Geographical location of company
- Geographical location of customer (same as company and/or different)

It is obvious that a for-profit company focuses on different issues than a charity or NGO, both of which tend to communicate with clients or volunteers. Such communication tends to differ a great deal in content and tone compared to a corporation's news feed. The size of the organization will also affect the depth and breadth of available social media know-how, as well as resources to perform these tasks.

Consumer products also require different use of social media tools and techniques than, for example, services. Depending upon location, consumers may prefer certain platforms over others to contact a brand (e.g., Facebook). Language may add another dimension to the communication if both the employee and your client use English as a third or fourth language, for instance. The potential for misunderstandings always increases when the parties trying to communicate do not share the same cultural context (i.e. idioms, slang, humour).

The above factors must be considered when conducting a social media audit in your organization, and considering these "variables" or factors makes an audit more comprehensive, if not complex. For instance, a larger company may use Facebook and Google+ for brands A, B, and so forth, each having a separate page on both platforms. Synergies might be realized. In contrast, for a small company, having a page on both Facebook and Google+ could already be too much to ask for.

3.2   Questions Your CEO Wants Answered

Unless you ask the social media experts conducting the audit about the following issues, they are unlikely to address them. The main reason for this possible oversight is that the questions posed below go beyond the classical audit mandate.

Nevertheless, you may want to address this with your top management team. If such questions are raised, you need to include them in the mandate you give to the experts conducting the social media audit, whether they be internal or external.

An overriding concern in the CEO's mind could be, *"How much can we improve return on investment (ROI)?"* To get a better idea or a partial answer for the CEO, the following issues should be investigated:

1. What *social media tools and activities* (e.g., Google+, LinkedIn) as well as *measuring and monitoring tools* (e.g., My.ComMetrics.com, Google Analytics) are *our competitors using with great success?* why and how?
2. *What social media benchmarks and elements* are other marketers testing and optimizing to maximize results?
3. Do we have *the proper resources (staffing and funding) in place* to best leverage our social media activities?
4. Yes, relevance is critical, but *what specific tactics are most effective* in determining relevancy for our company's or brand's target audience?
5. What is the *impact of using social media auditing information to further optimize social media activities as a percentage of revenue?*

6. What *impact does social media optimization have on priorities* like quote requests, free downloads, product sales, warranty work, recalls, and so forth?
7. *What opportunities are we missing* in social media optimization that should be explored to stay ahead of the competition?

Your auditor will be unable to give you a precise answer for some of these questions, especially if they come from outside your organisation. Nevertheless, the auditor may be able to help with some, such as questions 3, 4, and 5, and you can most likely provide the information for questions 6 and 7 yourself.

3.3   What the Social Media Auditor Needs from You

Cooperating with the auditors is a must since all of you are on the same side—client and auditor. Cooperation is essential to a successful social media audit.

The primary purpose of conducting routine social media audits is to identify opportunities for improvement that will help the company take better advantage of the possibilities, while using resources more effectively.

Acceptance that the team is responsible for creating and maintaining an effective system (*who is accountable for which activity*) within the company is a given. Establishment of such a system and the appropriate procedures is the responsibility of the organization and not the auditors.

The *people conducting your social media audit* will assist you in *identifying underperforming areas, as well as possible risk management and mitigation.* They will also provide suggestions and recommendations for correcting any issues that may come up.

In order for this excercise to run smoothly, you will need a *figure and table outlining which social media activities are handled by which department and individuals as well as an organization chart.* The assessor can then gain a better understanding of both your administrative and social media marketing structure, the nature of how you use these tools, as well as foster familiarity with the employees involved in this endeavor.

The Policy/procedure manual (if available) should be checked for completeness and provided ahead of the audit. We encourage all departments or smaller organizations to maintain a current manual covering subjects such as how to deal with policy violations. Procedures in case of a possible public relations crisis also must be addressed in the manual:

• Who will be contacted to coordinate the response to what (negative blog post somewhere, on company's Facebook Wall, call by journalist, etc.)?
• Which parties should be involved in preparing a response within 2 hours (even during public holidays)?
• Who will be responding on behalf of the organization?

This not only helps the social media auditors but, as importantly, facilitates the socialization of new employees and helps them find their way when they need help.

You need to *clear some workspace* for the social media auditors' use within reasonable proximity to the office staff and records that need to be accessed. The workspace should have adequate room and lighting. Depending on the situation, which may differ from one department to another, the space may be in use for a longer or shorter period of time.

The *social media audit staff should have authorized access* to any and all employees and records which may reasonably be necessary in the course of conducting the audit. The auditor's analysis of your social media marketing operation may require that several employees at various levels explain in detail how they perform their customer engagement, marketing, and other social media activities or tasks. In addition to examining hard copy records, it may be necessary for the auditor to make photocopies and/or obtain samples of key files for documentation. The auditor's access authority for computerised records is *Read Only*. The *confidentiality of records reviewed during the course of the audit* (i.e., financial and social media records/analyses) will be maintained by the auditor(s).

Expect an honest and candid appraisal of your social media marketing at the conclusion of the audit. The head of the department being audited will be provided with a Customer Satisfaction Survey. Each member of the audit staff has been professionally trained in the practice of internal auditing, and are expected to abide by both your own departmental standards, as well as the professional standards and ethics established by the Institute of Internal Auditors. Your objective answers and constructive comments on the survey form will assist the auditor in evaluating and improving the effectiveness of their program.

3.4   Preparing for the Audit with a Checklist

Whatever you do, *you need to document the answers to the questions below* and be able to show the team conducting the audit what you currently have in place including, if applicable, *what you have changed since the last audit* (i.e., improved upon).

Make sure that whenever the document for the auditors is updated, that is recorded accordingly. Hence, if the October preparations undertaken for the upcoming audit in January revealed some shortcomings, this needs to be added to the documentation. If you then decide to remedy the problem sometime in November, this must also be documented. For instance, what did you or the team do? How did this improve or eliminate the problem? Explain in a few sentences so the auditors can easily understand what happened.

An example could be that most comments left on Saturdays or Sundays where not published until they were reviewed on *Monday morning*. Due to this delay, you decided to change procedures. Starting November 15, one of your staff *now monitors comments during weekends and public holidays on a rotating schedule*. In practice, this means he or she checks Saturday and Sunday, mornings as well as evenings (e.g., 8:00 to 10:00 and 7:00 pm to 9:00 pm) for new comments posted by readers.

After checking for spam, comments are then released and replied to by the person approving the comment for publication. If she or he is not the author of the blog entry the reader left a comment on, she or he then informs the blog entry author via text message or phone call of the reader comment requiring a reply. The *author then has 24 hours to reply to the reader*.

The above procedure is what experts suggest be done in anticipation of a performance appraisal. Accordingly, before the actual appraisal, preliminary and informal feedback is given to the social media team regarding their performance, as it pertains to set objectives. Ideally, by the time the appraisal occurs, you will already have taken steps to improve the situation.

Preparing for a social media audit is similar, and if done early enough, this process provides information that can be discussed and learned from. Hopefully, changes will result in improvements before the actual audit. This also provides feedback from the auditors in case changes in performance have occurred, especially if these changes are in the right direction. Therefore, preparing for the audit offer the opportunity to do a kind of self-assessment and put the right changes in place before the actual review. This may still give the auditor a chance to point out certain things that warrant improvement. Nevertheless, this type of continuous development will be far more likely to show desirable results than a one-time affair each year, where one waits for the auditor and then lets the report he or she produced collect dust somewhere.

3.4.1   Regulation and Compliance Documentation

This information should confirm our compliance or log our non-compliance with relevant federal, state, and international laws and regulations. For instance, does your privacy policy address EU cookies regulations, do you use any software to collect statistics, such as Google Analytics, have an Adobe Flash presentation or execute any scripts (e.g., to show a number of images on your front page)?

Things that come to mind include privacy and data protection, e-commerce, and other pertinent regulations that you may have to adhere to locally (e.g., Switzerland), as well as any regulations pertaining to transactions with European consumers or US corporate clients.

Of course, if you have an incomplete privacy policy or lack social media guidelines for employees, please get one now, publish it online, and share with all employees.

How you record policy violations and what you do with this information is also important. For instance, how is such information used for education, thereby allowing employees to learn from mistakes? Proper record-keeping will also help further reduce the risk repeating mistakes in the future and your social media auditors will naturally also want to see it. However, this requires some funding in the budget to provide employee training that could help rectify issues outlined during the audit. Often we forget how quickly social media and IT technologies change, making it nearly impossible for staff to keep abreast new opportunities, options, and threats. It is not a good thing to expect that your employees understand Google's latest changes to its user privacy policy affecting the data stored regarding their use of YouTube, Gmail, Google+, searches, and so forth (ComMetrics, March 21, 2012). No can you expect staff to read up on the latest Facebook privacy changes (e.g., 34,000 words to read about changes on Facebook, see Gattiker, March 25, 2012).

Remember the KISS principle (Keep It Simple Stupid)—policies that do not fit on a cocktail napkin are often ignored by staff and users alike, so do not ask your lawyer to write these policies. In most cases, this will result in a long document that is too complex for the general user to comprehend. Get a non-lawyer to do it and ask your lawyer to review it if need be.

3.4.2 Outline Which Social Media Channels Are Used

This part of the documentation should *use a template* so the most pertinent information is listed in a similar way, regardless of the social media channel being referred to. This information has to be collected for each page on Facebook, Xing or LinkedIn, Twitter account or blog (e.g., customers vs. investors, see Dell), and provided to the auditors.

Information that you may want to include are when you established Facebook page(s), who the administrators are, and what objectives were set (what is the purpose of the page, value proposition, objectives, and benchmarks) For example, if the page is supposed to create comments, Likes, or other types of engagement, you need to spell out what satisfactory performance entails. Is it a quantitative measure, qualitative one, or a combination thereof? when do you post and why during those times and/or days? Maybe you post two to three times a week, particularly on Sunday mornings to increase the chances that corporate clients as well as consumers see these posts in their news stream (i.e., due to less new content, our chances of being seen in the stream are higher).

Talk with your staff; there might be *unauthorized Facebook pages* (e.g., https://www.facebook.com/MigrosIceTea?sk=info) and domains linked to your brand which you do not own (e.g., migrosicetea.ch = http://whois.domaintools.com/migrosicetea.ch).

Of course, there might be no need to shut them down or take them over either. Having product fans do the word-of-mouth marketing for you is a great asset. Nevertheless, such pages or a private blog about your products must be monitored (e.g., a user clips all news about a product and makes it accessible to the public - copyright issues? see http://www.memonic.com/user/alain/folder/migipedia. For instance, check the accuracy of Wall posts regarding this week's specials and inform the page owner if anything is incorrect or missing.

Finally, you want to check that the page's legal or site notice spells out who owns the page or domain. If the information is not listed, the page is non-compliant according to EU and Swiss law. Do not forget that a consumer may not immediately see that a Facebook page, such as https://www.facebook.com/MigrosIceTea?sk=info (fans of Migros Ice Tea), is not owned by the company. The above example neither lists the owner's name nor the ad agency's postal address as of May 2012, making the ad agency, as the page owner, noncompliant with Swiss law. Instead, it links to an official Migros page, possibly inadvertently giving an uninitiated consumer the impression that this it owned by the retailer. That cannot be in Migros best interests, can it?

3.4.3 Linking Offline and Online Marketing

It is important that we provide information regarding how offline and online marketing efforts are integrated with one another. In turn, it will be easier to demonstrate how you create synergies between the two, such as a print campaign and your iApp.

Make sure that the links provided on the Web site or blog relate to your product. In particular, there is no need to provide links that could be misconstrued as product endorsements.

The above indicates that we should clearly separate links to good causes that you sponsor, such as schools or charities, from those which are connected to any sort of payment (i.e. advertising). The same applies to the Web designer who put a link on your main page. Unless you agreed to this (remember you paid for his or her services), you should remove the link from this prime location.

3.4.4 Coherent Messaging Regardless of Channel

There must be a short summary explaining how you assure that your message is coherent and unifired across social media channels (e.g., multiple Twitter accounts or between Twitter and Google+).

This is not always the case, as outdoor equipment and clothing manufacturer Mammut has demonstrated. Mammut pursues an image as an environmentally responsible company. However, when the company decided to support a lobby group's efforts to get rid of a referendum on a CO_2 tax in Switzerland, its Facebook community was not amused (see http://commetrics.com/?p=16572/#comments).

Social media has given your clients a voice that can become very loud and very quickly spread a message, causing a lot of reputational damage. You need to be sure that there is no potential conflict of interest or confusing message(s) to your audience across various channels and media or they will stridently voice their disagreement on various Web 2.0 channels (Gattiker, September 6, 2011).

Therefore, ensure that your message is consistent and if it fails to be, determine why this happened and how this risk can be better managed next time.

3.4.5   *Information About Monitoring*

The auditor must receive information about who monitors which social media channel during weekends and public holidays. If attacks are launched, it generally happens before the weekend. Activists love long weekends because many companies are understaffed, and cannot respond adequately. However, if the company has a procedure in place and monitors what is happening, it should be fine.

Unfortunately, there are numerous examples of various companies failing to monitor their channels after Friday afternoon. As a result, the avalanche of negative publicity took on a life of its own and was so big by Monday morning, little could be done to rectify the situation (see —Nestlé KitKat and Greenpeace under Tuesday http://commetrics.com/?p=8802).

Therefore, an organization is well advised to use a rotating schedule, whereby six or eight employees share the job of monitoring your Facebook page or mentions on Twitter and Google+ on weekends. These employees may be the same that monitor blog comments and reply to comments left on your Google+ or Facebook page.

3.5   Checklist Rating for the CyTRAP Social Media Audit Toolkit

In the preceding section, I outlined the issues that warrant addressing before the auditors show up on your premises. Particularly important is discussing these issues with your team and documenting what you have implemented. As important, check a month or so before the formal audit process starts whether the new procedures are working properly. Document any insights gained during this process and use findings to help staff learn and improve performance.

In subsequent chapters we present *templates and checklists to assist you with conducting a social media audit in your organization*. The tools are prepared and set up in such a way that they can easily be adjusted to your specific needs. In turn, you can go into more or less detail depending upon the size, complexity, and industry of your organization.

The biggest challenge is that *rules that are too specific will create a check-box mentality*, whereby people will do exactly what is required, but no more or less. Many things regarding social media, such as how we prepare for a public relations disaster, can be accomplished in several different ways. It is not always obvious which will be the best approach. Because tools and situations change so fast, it is difficult to predict and forecast. For instance, who is to say that Pinterest will not be used in 18 months' time to launch an attack against some brands?

3.5.1   Compliance Is Not Always Compliance

Compliance is about running a business and delivering products in ways that are fair and ethical.

Compliance is an attempt to ensure that products and services benefit both the provider and the user. Following the spirit as well as the letter of the law is the key to successful compliance (see social media policy resource page http://info.cytrap. eu/?page_id=686).

Using social media and interacting with customers and suppliers through social networks, communities, or blogs *entails risks regarding reputation management, trade secrets, and so on, which need to be managed.* The right controls and systems must also be put into place. As important, how well these work in practice must be regularly reviewed in order to know whether things are working properly (for more, see http://info.cytrap.eu/?page_id=83).

The *CyTRAP Social Media Audit Toolkit (CySoMAT) is a systematic method that covers common social media regulations and best practices* necessary for an enterprise to *establish a baseline level of performance, expose high-risk areas, safeguard intellectual property, and ensure legal compliance.* The CySoMAT facilitates a *principle-based approach to the social media audit* that requires *exercising good judgment, doing the "right" thing, and ethical conduct,* even if neither the law nor the company's social media guidelines are specific enough. It also *encourages the better use of tools and scarce resources* (e.g., staff) to better leverage social media efforts to *serve clients better.* The latter is achieved by *focusing on a better customer experience.*

3.5.2   How the CyTRAP Social Media Audit Tool Works

The CySoMAT provides an easy-to-understand roadmap that allows companies to intelligently navigate the ocean of social media challenges. To ensure consideration of the worst-case scenario, we have emphasized the requirements for SMEs, however the CySoMAT is applicable to organizations of all sizes and types, whether industry, government, or non-profit.

The social media audit program presented in subsequent chapters alongside the CySoMAT provides corporate executives, as well as financial and technical management and personnel, with a *pragmatic map for action.* In order to *ascertain the internal controls and to facilitate the corporate board's assessment of potential compliance threats* affecting strategic objectives, the CySoMAT offers a rated list of practical procedures to ensure effective use of social media opportunities. Documenting and auditing social media procedures and reporting findings to the shareholders and regulators is typically required by business accountability legislation, such as the Sarbanes–Oxley Act (US), Realignment of the Swiss CO—Art 727 CO (Art 728a Para 1 Nr. 3 CO), or KonTrag (Germany).

Unfortunately, in this context "Pragmatic" means that our template and audit process tools are not for use by ose companies that need it most. An example might be the executive whose use of Web 2.0 and social media applications and tools are not up to par or cause problems. They are typically in denial and cannot be helped.

Rather the template will be most helpful to those executives that are already fully committed to using social media and its marketing methods and would implement Web 2.0 or 3.0 solutions anyway. The difference is that by using our tools and templates *they can achieve effective and strategic implementation and improvements faster, easier, and less expensively.*

Table 3.1 outlines our straightforward rating system and provides an interpretation of each of these scales.

3.5.2.1   How the Rating Scale Works

The rating scale provided in Table 3.1 provides a ranking system ranging from low to severe (e.g., high risk, not legally compliant, possible privacy, and/or copyright violations, as well as liability issues). The company will have to determine what group of questions (see Tables in subsequent chapters) warrants priority 1 or 2, etc.

Each question's score can then be multiplied by the score given by the auditors for the item in question. Based on the priority rankings, you know what the maximum number is and can compare that to your achieved score.

The *checklist can help arrange and conduct broad social media process assessments*, with the social media auditors identifying the areas with weak or inadequate corporate controls, or where violation of laws and regulations is possible. The *first type* of audit would focus on the structure and operation of social media processes and systems. The *second type* would provide the stakeholders with an overview of how well a corporation is self-policing its social media activities and whether it is fully compliant with the privacy, financial accounting, and other pertinent laws and regulations.

Our checklist is hardly a legal document. However, it is intended to help SMEs and other organizations achieve best practices for using social media marketing tools and methods for leveraging resources to better serve customers.

3.6   Conclusion

To address the letter and the spirit of the law, we have instituted four questions for most settings in which we have been asked to help with social media guidelines, their administration and audits.

When one is faced with an ethical problem or a difficult situation on the social Web, our social media guidelines suggest that you ask yourself these four questions before going ahead and sharing:

Table 3.1 Rating scale for social media audit and appraisal

Star rating	Priority	Description
*****	Severe	High risk (e.g., reputation, regulation, customer satisfaction), fixing this matter entails substantial costs, however, may be necessary to maintain legal compliance
****	Critical	Risk management, liability, and regulatory demands make this a short-term priority (e.g., gaining competitive advantage)
***	Essential	As essential as the higher ratings and considered to illustrate best practice; competitor is exploring the same or similar
**	Elevated	Implementation needed to achieve performance objectives set for social media activities
*	Low	Nice to use or have implemented if resources permit

Note: The biggest challenge is avoiding the trap of a check-box mentality, whereby people will do exactly what is required, but no more or less. Accordingly, scoring your social media efforts during the audit is not a black or white affair, but *numerous shades of gray that may require discussions and explanations for others to understand the challenges and consequences of doing things a certain way*

- Would I consider it personally embarrassing or unpleasant if my colleagues heard about this (e.g., tweet, blog comment)?
- Could I be considered to have unfairly benefitted from this activity due solely to my organizational position?
- Could my company's reputation suffer if the media or competitors get hold of this?
- Could the client, friend, or foe be upset by receiving my tweet, e-mail, or comment on Google+ for instance because they feel talked down to or brushed off?

Policy and compliance management is a process, not an event (for more, see http://info.cytrap.eu/?page_id=83). The increasingly difficult regulatory regime makes it a core organizational principle, which must be adopted and incorporated into our daily working environment.

This chapter has provided the reader with some tips and hints regarding how to prepare for an upcoming audit of the company's social media marketing. The CyTRAP Social Media Audit Tool (CySoMAT) was presented and a possible rating scale for social media audit and appraisal given. The latter outlined rankings from low through elevated, essential, critical and severe priority that could be used in the upcoming templates for your audit.

Chapter 4 will discuss the scope and focus of the social media audit. By defining this, you not only help the auditor focus on the things that matter to you, but also allow your staff to focus on the same. Accordingly, giving the audit the wrong parameters will not help your staff become more effective. Chapter 4 discusses these challenges in some depth.

References

Commetrics (March 21, 2012). Google privacy policy vs. Article 29 Working Party. [Google Plus Page—ComMetrics] Retrieved March 29, 2012 from https://plus.google.com/b/103400392486480765286/103400392486480765286/posts/CDjWRL1oeff

Gattiker, Urs. E. (March 25, 2012). Facebook und Google: 7 Tipps und Tools zum besseren Datenschutz (Facebook and Google: 7 tips and tools to better protect your privacy). [Blog post - CyTRAP]. Retrieved March 29, 2012 from http://info.cytrap.eu/?p=3621

Gattiker, Urs E. (September 6, 2011). Why become a guest blogger? (transparency, conflict of interest issues—Federal Trade Commission guides) [Blog post—ComMetrics]. Retrieved January 10, 2012 from http://commetrics.com//?page_id=91

Chapter 4
Scope and Focus of the Social Media Audit

Abstract Preparing for an audit (e.g., checking for documentation and its completeness) is critical, as outlined in Chapter 3. However, before we embark on this important exercise and start with our social media audit, we need to define the scope (e.g., how in-depth, and the focus must be agreed upon, such as Facebook, Twitter, and blog activities or something else. This chapter addresses these issues and provides some guidance.

Recently, I did a security and privacy audit for a hospital, and defining the scope, breadth, and depth of the audit was difficult. In fact, most of the checklists I had in order to conduct this work systematically were used, but never presented to top management. Instead, the latter described in general terms what they wanted from us. The idea was for a general overview (what I call a light audit) to identify some structural and possibly major issues. In turn, the CEO then decided that some things would be investigated in more depth once he had seen the management letter with a table outlining the major concerns.

The audit checklist presented in this book covers common social media regulations and best practices that are necessary for an enterprise to establish a baseline level of performance, expose high-risk areas, safeguard intellectual property, and ensure legal compliance.

As we pointed out earlier, the social media audit is an objective assurance and consulting activity. It is designed to add value and improve an organization's social media operations.

A systematic, disciplined approach to evaluating and improving the effectiveness of risk management, compliance, and governance helps the organization review and improve its performance as far as social media marketing is concerned.

Below we discuss how you can define the scope and outline the particulars of the social media audit you intend to conduct in your organization.

U.E. Gattiker, *Social Media Audit: Measure for Impact*, SpringerBriefs
in Computer Science, DOI 10.1007/978-1-4614-3603-4_4, © The Author(s) 2013

4.1   Scope of the Social Media Audit

Table 4.1 outlines the issues that need to be specified before you conduct an audit. The audit could be more or less extensive depending upon the context and size of the organization. For instance, if you have brand pages on Facebook (e.g., Magnum Ice Cream) you may audit the "Facebook process" that includes but is not limited to such things as how:

- Content is prepared.
- Engagement and interaction is monitored.
- Whatever else you deem important.

Furthermore, you may assess how your Facebook pages are managed across countries and/or languages. To illustrate, Magnum Ice Cream's Facebook pages are managed by different teams across countries, a very logical approach. However, this also means that each group handles things a bit differently and has to deal with different issues in Germany versus the UK for example.

You may also have to *assess performance across channels such as Facebook and/or Twitter, your corporate blogs, Google+*, etc. Nevertheless, you can *use the same tables and forms for each of these social media networks.*

Table 4.1 Scope of social media audit

Name of organization being audited	Address of organization being audited
…………..	…………..
Social media process(es) being audited	Social media platforms included (e.g., Facebook, Twitter, Quora, LinkedIn, Xing, Viadeo, Second Life, Skype, blog)
…………..	…………..
Process supplier—internal and outsourced (e.g., tools, software , staff time, technical skills, and other departments)	Customers of the output generated- internal and external clients
…………..	…………..
Inputs (e.g., research, writing, editing, and video editing)	List of outputs produced by this process (e.g., tweets, blog posts, blog comments and replies, e-mail responses, social bookmarking, and internal and external clients)
…………..	…………..
Compliance	Internal control system (ICS)
Must the social media audit report in some way reporting to another auditing process as required by law or regulation (e.g., Sarbanes–Oxley and KonTrag)?	Does the work in some way address an area as listed in your ICS to better manage risk? could it be that ICS-related work identified issues regarding IT use/social media applications that need to be addressed?
…………..	…………..
Notes and comments about the scope of the audit	
…………..	

Note: The above table contains information needed to better understand the focus of the audit

Accordingly, you can do the social media audit for a Facebook page, Twitter account, and corporate blog together using the forms and checklists we provide below. If you prefer, you can do each separately.

Table 4.1 collects some of the basic information that is needed before you embark on an audit regarding social media marketing efforts in your organization.

The issues addressed in Table 4.1 ask you to define which process is being audited, as well as who will be the recipient of the output produced by the audit, and which platforms should be assessed. The type of input that will be used such as internal reports, industry research, or university research is outlined and specified. The more detailed this information, the easier will it be to conduct the audit by evaluating exactly those things the company would like scrutinized.

The forms, including Table 4.1, are such that each category can easily be expanded by adding another line for text. The more specific the instructions, the faster the audit can be conducted and the less likely there will be any misunderstandings that could delay the process unnecessarily.

As suggested in Table 4.1, it is equally important that you note whether compliance or governance issues pertaining to the use of social media or privacy legislation potentially requiring further investigation have been raised by other parties, such as your financial auditors. Similar things apply for the internal control system that addresses risk issues pertaining to financial matters and operational processes including IT infrastructure and software. All these may mention social media marketing or the use of social networks being a risk. If others have raised issues related to social media marketing and social networks, then they need to be spelled out here so the social media auditor can address them and provide you with information necessary for responding to compliance and governance matters.

In short, the *scope of the audit has to be defined.* Table 4.1 is a first step indicating that we need to discuss and internally agree upon the *scope* (how much depth is required?), *breadth* (how wide will our net be?), *and depth* (how much detail is needed?) *of the audit* required in order to achieve our objectives (see also introduction to Chapter 7).

4.2   Profile and Particulars of the Social Media Audit

In Table 4.2 we outline what other information must be provided to simplify the systematic approach to conducting an audit. Issues that must be spelled out include:

- Who owns the process
- Who will actually conduct the audit

Of course, the schedule for the audit and those that review the audit results (e.g., management group) must be spelled out. This will help focus the audit to provide the information the stakeholder wants to see from this exercise.

To avoid misunderstandings it is also advisable to address the plan, and how the company or audit team will proceed when conducting the social media audit.

Table 4.2 Profile and particulars of social media audit

Brief description of the plan for the social media audit	
…………..	
Auditees	
Process owner	Human resources and/or staff who work with the process (e.g., those tweeting on behalf of the organization)
…………..	…………..
Social media auditors	
Audit manager	Audit staff
……………	…………..
Audit schedule	
Audit start date (20 yr-m-d)	Audit finish date (20 yr-m-d)
…………..	…………..
Review of audit	
Audit reviewed by	Date the audit review was performed
…………..	…………..
Inputs	List of outputs produced by this process
(e.g., research, writing, editing, and video editing)	(e.g., tweets, blog posts, blog comments and replies, e-mail responses, social bookmarking, and internal and external clients)
…………..	…………..
Notes and comments about the scope of the audit	
…………..	

Note: The above table contains information regarding staff, timing, and scheduling of the various tasks to be undertaken during the audit

Of course, who will conduct the audit needs to be specified, as does the recipient of the output. Again, the more carefully this is addressed by the team, the more details and specifics can be provided. This helps auditors deliver information the client needs sooner. An audit report that provides the information needed for making strategic decisions while eliminating regulatory and compliance-related concerns empowers the client to improve subsequent performance.

4.3   Conclusion

While an audit is an important assessment, ultimately it should enable the company to perform better. Higher performance will then help increase customer loyalty, specifically client satisfaction. While the satisfied customer may talk about their satisfaction with five others, the unsatisfied person talks about their dissatisfaction to nine or more people. This is word-of-mouth marketing at its worst.

Unfortunately, when we start a social media advertising campaign, such as a sponsored tweet, only approximately four percent of those dissatisfied with our product or campaign will talk to us. An example illustrating this challenge was

McDonalds' advertising campaign on Twitter during January 2012. A few things went wrong and the archived material shows how an audit can help you prepare for these kinds of situations (see http://www.flickr.com/photos/cytrap/6925148273/).

However, in order to provide us with the information we need to succeed when such a situation occurs, or to improve how we manage our social media activities, the *scope and focus of our audit must be defined* beforehand. Like an information security audit or a privacy audit, the social media audit will reveal more or less depending on the *scope (how much depth is required?), breadth (how wide will our net be?), and depth (how much detail is needed?) we require* of the audit. Of course, the more scope, breadth, and depth we want, the more time and human resources will be required, also increasing expense (see also introduction to Chapter 7 for more information).

The templates in this chapter help address scope, breadth, and depth issues. If necessary, the tables in subsequent chapters can be adjusted and fewer questions can be addressed. In turn, the methods presented fit the organizational context by making it feasible to adjust the templates to your needs.

Chapter 5 will provide some tools and templates that help structure the audit process as well as manage it effectively.

Chapter 5
Development and Management of the Process

Abstract Chapter 4 provided some templates for defining the scope and focus of the social media audit. Chapter 5 outlines how the audit process can be developed and managed effectively. The checklists, templates, and questions will guide the reader through the pertinent issues. The process begins with focusing on strategy and staff resources, then moves on to compliance matters measuring and monitoring challenges. The chapter continues discussing how to evaluate what skills the company has available for social media marketing. It wraps it up with addressing disaster management and highlighting matters concerning the value proposition of using social media as a company, non-profit, or government agency.

5.1 Introduction

The CySoMAT covers common social media regulations and best practices that are necessary for an enterprise to establish a baseline level of performance, expose high-risk areas, safeguard intellectual property, and ensure legal compliance. It is a template applying fact-based, structured techniques to the appraisal of the organization's social media activities and customer relationship efforts.

Each of the points listed in the tables can be given a priority weight. As outlined in Table 3.1, these are:

- 5 star = severe
- 4 star = critical
- 3 star = essential
- 2 star = elevated
- 1 star = low

U.E. Gattiker, *Social Media Audit: Measure for Impact*, SpringerBriefs   43
in Computer Science, DOI 10.1007/978-1-4614-3603-4_5, © The Author(s) 2013

Table 5.1 Basic issues that must be addressed and understood to steer the ship and stay on course

#	Rating	Policy and strategy	Points
5.1.1	*****	Was the purpose of using social media for the organization spelled out (e.g., one-page document that uses plain language) (see also Table 5.6)?	0, 1, 2, or 3
5.1.2	*****	Was social media's value proposition discussed and spelled out (i.e., one page stating, for instance, we use it to serve customers better by doing as follows..., see also Table 1.1)?	...
5.1.3	*****	Has a strategy for social media activities been developed?	...
5.1.4	*****	Did management approve a budget for this process (e.g., budget includes fixed, variable, overhead, and labor costs)?	...
5.1.5	*****	Did top management address how it wants social media to support key drivers (e.g., customer satisfaction, returns, sales growth) for the next period (e.g., quarter and/or business year)?	...
5.1.6	*****	Has the person responsible for and reporting to management about this process been identified?	...

Note: As outlined in Table 3.1, each item can be ranked according to priority ranging from 5 stars = Severe priority, to 1 star = Low priority rating. Ranking will depend upon context (e.g., industry, country) and size of business

Each issue listed above was given a 5, the highest priority, because unless these issues have been fully addressed and management has agreed it will be difficult to steer the ship in the right direction while performing satisfactorily

Each activity in the table can then be given points according to the progress made: 0 = not addressed, 1 = some work done, 2 = organizational guidelines and policies being met, 3 = being compliant—meeting regulatory standards and/or having done a thorough job

The total number of points can range from 0 to 3 for each item, which is then multiplied by the number of stars given, ranging from 1 to 5. The range of scores for each item is therefore 0 to 15, which is then multiplied by the number of questions. Accordingly, for the above table, the maximum score is 6 (questions) × 15 = 90

What is priority will change based on various factors. For instance, the maturity model (see Table 1.2) already suggests that depending upon your company's situation its approach to an audit will differ significantly. To illustrate, the adopter will probably have taken care of managing the policy and strategy process a while back (see Table 5.1). Nevertheless, a reevaluation might be advisable since things change very fast. For instance, in 2008, Friend Feed was a popular platform that got a lot of attention and was used by most social media pundits. In 2011, Facebook took over the platform and since then it has become rather quiet this means that while we may have wanted to use it in 2009 or 2010, the wisdom of spending resources to actively manage this channel in 2012 or 2013 is questionable.

A person or entity categorised as an adopter on the maturity model (see Table 1.2) might also put a great deal of attention on monitoring and measuring (Table 5.2), as

Table 5.2 Measuring and monitoring

#	Rating	Measuring for impact	Points
5.2.1	*****	Output requirements from stakeholder (e.g., management, clients, regulators, and suppliers), such as what is *appropriate* engagement (e.g., proper tweet or good blog comment on corporate blog or client's/other party's Web site), have been defined and shared with employees	0, 1, 2, or 3
5.2.2	*****	Output requirements from stakeholder (e.g., management, clients, regulators, and suppliers), such as *frequency of engagement*, have been defined/spelled out and shared with employees	…
5.2.3	*****	Documentation regarding how process personnel communicates with those that depend upon its output has been defined/spelled out in detail	…
5.2.4	*****	Documentation about how process personnel communicates with those parties that supply them with input (e.g., information about a research report that is being released by a staff group) is defined	…
5.2.5	*****	A plan regarding what type of measurement methods will be used to demonstrate that process outputs meet requirements has been developed	…
5.2.6	*****	A way to monitor the quality of outputs (e.g., monitoring tone or sentiment of responses, brand mentions) has been selected and put in place	…
5.2.7	*****	Measurement methods that show how this process is capable of achieving planned results (see also Q 5.7.3) have been selected and put in place	…

Note: The total number of points can range from 0 to 3 for each item, which is then multiplied by the number of stars given, ranging from 1 to 3. The range of scores for each item is therefore 0 to 15, which is then multiplied by the number of questions. Accordingly, for the above table, the maximum score is 7 (questions) × 15 = 105
For more information about the calculations, scaling, and rationale, please see Table 5.1

well as a disaster management plan (see Table 5.3), since many large organizations that use social media extensively still have many difficulties finding the right metrics to properly evaluate their performance (e.g., see https://plus.google.com/113060135338232163785/posts/eFzurCXEPpy).

Each activity being assessed in the tables presented can then be scored according to the progress made on the following scale:

- 0 = not addressed
- 1 = some work done
- 2 = organizational guidelines and policies being met
- 3 = being compliant—meeting regulatory standards

Table 5.3 Disaster management

#	Rating	Preparing for a crisis	Points
5.3.1	*****	A thorough disaster management plan has been developed (yes or no)	0, 1, 2, or 3
5.3.2	*****	The disaster plan identifies who must be informed using which channels (e.g., mobile and/or stationary phone) within what time frame to coordinate the response (i.e., disaster management officer is contacted within 30 minutes; the officer then contacts the appropriate parties within a further 30 minutes)	...
5.3.3	*****	The disaster plan stipulates acceptable response time (e.g., during weekends, Christmas, or summer holidays), in case of, for example, a: –Negative wall post on company's Facebook page (or elsewhere about company or its brand); the item is replied to within 2 hours, providing the facts that show how the commenter/client may be either misinformed or correct	...
5.3.4	*****	The disaster plan document addresses what is considered a serious issue and what is not, including giving examples illustrating the matter for employees	...
5.3.5	*****	Templates for appropriate replies (e.g., tweets, e-mail, Facebook wall) are provided to acknowledge receipt and inform the other party that the matter is being investigated promptly	...
5.3.6	*****	If necessary, a procedure is outlined on how matters can and should be followed up to ensure the client received not only a reply (e.g., if passed to another department), but one that was satisfactory and within the time rame stipulated by the disaster management plan	...
5.3.7	*****	The disaster management plan has been tested (i.e., a fire drill was done) within the last 12 months and results show that response procedures and processes are followed correctly by staff	...

Note: The total number of points can range from 0 to 3 for each item, which is then multiplied by the number of stars given, ranging from 1 to 5. The range of scores for each item is therefore 0 to 15, which is then multiplied by the number of questions. Accordingly, for the above table, the maximum score is 7 (questions) × 15 = 105
For more information about the calculations, scaling, and rationale, please see Table 5.1

In cases where the above scale warrants changing, a note at the bottom of each table usually outlines the amendments. This should make it easier for those being presented with the findings to also understand the meaning of data presented in each table or portion of the report.

Finally, the total score for each table can then computed. For instance, if we have ten items, each of which received 3 points and a rating of 5 stars (severe priority), the maximum score for each item would be 15. Therefore, the score for the table would be 150 (10 items × 3 points × 5 stars).

Of course, you may add or delete questions as you see fit, and, some issues you may not want to address. These tables and checklists are to be used as a drawing board to be revised, improved, shortened, and so on to make them work best in your context. You may choose to select a few tables only and leave the rest. No problem, each template is set up to work perfectly on its own. Simply adjust the process to make it fit the scope and depth you need according to your size of organization, budget, and brands.

5.2   Policy and Strategy

Policy is a blueprint of the organizational activities which are likely more repetitive or routine in nature. Examples include an absence policy or a customer return policy, which outlines when and how people can return products after Christmas. For instance, the company may have decided to take products back without a receipt, for which customers are then given a store credit.

By contrast, *strategy is concerned with those organizational decisions which have not been dealt with before in the same form.* Accordingly, social media policy may outline done and not done with the corporate Twitter account, while strategy is the methodology used to achieve the objective as prescribed by the policy.

In Table 5.1, each activity is given the highest priority because without strategy and policy we would be like a ship without navigation. Also, the person coordinating and responsible for the process has been identified. Nevertheless, you are free to change these ratings as you see fit. In fact, you may provide your auditor with guidance regarding the priority rating or let them make that decision for you based on their findings and insights.

5.3   Resources and Staff

In Table 5.4, questions posted raise the issues of availability of necessary resources. These can range from employees' time requirements to tools for performing their tasks. An example might be having access to a URL shortener that allows scheduling of tweets and so forth.

Other questions that need addressing consist of who will be tweeting on the company's behalf or updating the Facebook page and replying to comments made by fans.

Who tweets on the company's Twitter account must be determined and those people's job descriptions have to reflect these additional duties. As well, what satisfactory performance entails while doing these duties, such as replying to a blog comment, needs to be spelled out. Those *employees' annual performance review should include a social media component.*

Table 5.4 Setting the foundation for managing the process effectively

#	Rating	Resources, stuff, and tools for activities	Points
5.4.1	*****	Employees working with social media (e.g., tweeting, writing blog posts, replying to comments on Facebook) have been identified	0, 1, 2, or 3
5.4.2	*****	Time budget: hours required to satisfactorily perform these social media activities have been made part of the budget (see also points 5.4.1 and 5.4.4)	...
5.4.3	*****	Financial budget: besides labor costs (see point 5.4.2), expenses for software, internet connection and hardware, as well as a cost-benefit analysis (see Chapter 2, Tables 2.1–2.6) are in place to achieve the objectives set	...
5.4.4	*****	The job descriptions of those employees identified under point 5.4.1 reflect these changes, and their performance appraisal includes a social media component	...
5.4.5	*****	The best engagement times for reaching our target audience have been identified (e.g., tweet regularly between Monday and Friday, once at 7:00 am, and/or once in the afternoon local time)	...
5.4.6	*****	Policy has been established regarding our response to comments on blog(s) or community forum(s) (on Web site or discussion group on Xing, LinkedIn). For instance, 95% of the time our staff replies to these within 12 hours, 7 days a week (including Christmas and summer holidays)	...
5.4.7	*****	The tool used for monitoring Twitter has been identified (replies on Twitter, people tweeting our blog posts)	...
5.4.8	*****	Two tools that can be used as URL shorteners (e.g., for Twitter, to track clicks) have been identified and are used in-house (i.e., not using overlay toolbar, see http://commetrics.com/?p=15286/#comment-299737123)	...
5.4.9	*****	Process for who posts updates (responsibilities) on various platforms is in place (e.g., wall post or note on Facebook, LinkedIn group, blog entries)	...
5.4.10	*****	Process to monitor and follow up on requests for quotes and information is in place For instance, e-mail is passed on to expert, who replies with a cc to original recipient of request (e.g., communication department). Original recipient follows up with e-mail to original sender to see if expert's reply resolved client's issue. In 95% of cases, clients get a reply within 24 hours, Monday through Sunday including public holidays	...

Note: Total number of points can range from 0 to 3 for each item, which is then multiplied by the number of stars given, ranging from 1 to 5. The range of scores for each item is therefore 0 to 15, which is then multiplied by the number of questions. Accordingly, for the above table, the maximum score is 10 (questions) × 15 = 150

For more information about the calculations, scaling, and rationale, please see Table 5.1

Furthermore, Table 5.4 also lists some issues pertaining to the budget necessary to pay for the hours used to perform the tasks required. *Unless these resources are put in place*, satisfactory performance will be a near impossibility. This includes resources for purchasing the tools and services needed, including outsourcing some things if the expertise is not available in-house.

5.4 Managing Compliance and Risks

Unless your staff is aware of compliance risks and necessary documentation has been put in place, it will be very difficult to show regulators or other stakeholders that the company is compliant. For instance, if users can register themselves, we need to make sure that privacy regulations are strictly adhered to. Also, if users contact the company via social media, such as Twitter, policies pertaining to their privacy rights must be adhered to by each employee.

In principle, *social media marketing must deal with three risks:*

1. *Lack of strategy* (see also Chapter 1), meaning the company has not clearly spelled out the purpose of using social media nor how it intends to achieve what objectives.
2. *Overreliance on technology*, meaning the company relies on software tools such as Hubspot, Radian6, or My.ComMetrics.com to do their social media marketing. All three are excellent tools when used by trained people operating under the direction of a corporate strategy that outlines what goals must be accomplished (e.g., SMART (specific, manageable, actionable, relevant, trending) metrics including key drivers that measurement must focus on).
3. *Proliferation of social media marketing*, meaning different social media marketing efforts that blur brand image and may damage the firm's reputation (e.g., large firms average about 93 different social media accounts). This requires quality assurance with a social media audit, whereby processes are reviewed systematically. Results will show where the firm falls short, as well as where things can be improved and how.

Table 5.5 outlines some of the most obvious obstacles that we must address to minimize the risk of failure while still making it possible to manage the aim is to use the discussions needed to address issues listed in Table 5.5 in such a way that we can estimate what it is worth spending to protect ourselves against said issues.

There are opportunity costs in failing to confront uncertainty (e.g., Woo, 2011). Of course, this might necessitate some additional training for staff to ensure they understand the possible risks and how these can be measured effectively. Also, unless a privacy officer has been identified and this function is clearly separated from system administration, as well as the security or risk function, we are likely to fail the compliance test on privacy issues alone.

Table 5.5 Compliance, governance, and risk management

#	Rating	Ensuring that what works in theory works in practice	Points
5.5.1	*****	The company has social media guidelines in plain language that are relatively short (i.e., fit on a napkin) (resource page: http://info.cytrap.eu/?page_id=686)	0, 1, 2, or 3
5.5.2	*****	Regulatory developments affecting social media and Web 3.0 use (e.g., EU cookie law versus use of flash on Web pages) are implemented as required by law	...
5.5.3	*****	The necessary records are identified in order to *monitor compliance*; an example might be records that list when, where, and by whom social media guidelines were violated during the last period. Violations are discussed with the transgressor and consequences or risks are laid out for employees to see	...
5.5.4	*****	The necessary records have been identified (see point 5.5.3) in order to *control for compliance* (e.g., doing unannounced spot checks of whether a clean desk policy is being followed throughout the organization) and regular reviews of these violations are in place	...
5.5.5	*****	Staff understands which rules need to be adhered to when engaging with clients on social media (e.g., being courteous, possible liability issues) and regular review of these violations are in place	...
5.5.6	*****	Staff understands what kind of risks they are exposed to when exchanging tweets, Facebook posts, or replying to a reader's comment on the corporate blog and regular reviews of these violations are in place	...
5.5.7	*****	Staff know which compliance issues they must consider and be careful about when sharing information (e.g., trade secret, issues identified by regulator as problematic such as possible sharing of insider information) and regular reviews of these violations are in place	...
5.5.8	*****	Risks regarding privacy and data protection have been identified (e.g., getting user account to download document) and regular reviews of these violations are in place	...

Note: The total number of points can range from 0 to 3 for each item, which is then multiplied by the number of stars given, ranging from 1 to 5. The range of scores for each item is therefore 0 to 15, which is then multiplied by the number of questions. Accordingly, for the above table, the maximum score is 8 (questions) $\times$ 15 = 120

For more information about the calculations, scaling, and rationale, please see Table 5.1

5.5   Measuring and Monitoring

When you put the process in place, you are likely not yet fully aware of what and how to measure. Some obvious things that you may want to measure are page views or unique visitors. Many large companies do just that. However, such easy-to-get measures—sometimes called the low-hanging fruit of social media—do not always provide us with the insight we need to determine how effective our performance is.

Unless we use collected information for clearly specified purposes, we must question why we collect the data. For instance, monitoring brand mentions for your company is a nice exercise, but may soon deteriorate into pure navel-gazing. To prevent this, it is necessary to determine what will be done with such mentions, both positive and negative. Will you contact each author of a negative mention to collect more information and hopefully fix their problem in the process? Or will you just report the number and indicate that since it is lower than last period we are doing fine?

At this stage, however, we are more concerned about what is appropriate engagement and what is not (see Table 5.2). Similar to exhibiting the right manners on the telephone (e.g., how to pick up and answer, how to deal with an irate client), off-the-cuff remarks are inappropriate. Also, mistakenly posting a personal comment on the organization's Twitter account or Facebook page can happen, but should not. Nevertheless, unless employees understand the issue and you monitor for such mishaps, this is a risk that could result in a public relations nightmare (Gattiker, Urs E. April 4, 2011).

5.6 Human Capital

Of course, the right human resources need to be in place to use social media effectively. What makes this a real challenge is that things evolve relatively quickly, so your social media expert(s) will have to spend considerable time staying abreast of new developments. At its best, Continuing education means you are pretty well informed about changes and what a new tool such as Google+ versus Facebook or Viadeo versus Xing means for your organization.

Worst is when things move so fast that you are still dreaming about Beebo or Second Life—the virtual community—when your clients have already moved on to Renfren (China's Twitter).

Your employees are your biggest asset when it comes to social media. To begin with, each has their own network of strong (e.g., family and close friends) and weak ties (acquaintances). Furthermore, each may already be active on several platforms, and therefore have the ability to help monitor the social Web and comment on people's blog entries or Facebook postings regarding topics of interest to both themselves and the company and/or its products. As such, your staff are important multipliers. However, in order to have their activities benefit them and sometimes also their employer and colleagues, you need to provide them with chances to refine their skills, acquire new ones and feel comfortable with things you work with.

For instance, when Google+ was still relatively new to the scene at the end of 2011, we provided some training sessions for in-house, as well as clients, allowing them to learn how to use Google+ features to their greatest advantage while simultaneously managing search engine optimization (SEO). The training aspect is one area that often gets overlooked. Put differently, your staff may need some upgrading when it comes to regulatory changes and tools in accounting, law, and compliance. The same applies for social media networking and tools. Simply providing such training to management is not recommended as a viable strategy. Finally, during such sessions, many employees benefit from each other's talents and you may be surprised what talent and human capital is in the audience. This must be leveraged wisely.

5.6.1 Disaster Management

When people think of disaster, they usually think of:

- Natural disasters (e.g., floods, earthquakes)
- Environmental emergencies (e.g., industrial accidents, usually involving hazard-ous material)
- Complex emergencies (e.g., breakdown of authority, such as rioting and looting)
- Pandemic emergencies (e.g., sudden onset of a contagious disease)

In these contexts, disaster can disrupt the provision of services such as health care, drinking water, and garbage collection, increasing the risk of undesirable out-comes. For instance, not collecting garbage increases the risk of the spread of dis-ease. If during a heat wave the electricity supply fails people may die due to heat exhaustion.

Governments may also want to use social media during disasters. They have already begun using social media to quickly help them spread information to the public, collect information regarding the extent of a disaster, and prioritize relief efforts (Gattiker, Urs E. August 25, 2010).

However, in the context of this book disaster *refers to cases where social media may help information that could damage a company's brand and reputation go viral.* For instance, when *Greenpeace attacked Nestlé for its use of palm oil*, the company took too long to educate the public via Facebook and YouTube about its activities. Providing such information in a more timely manner could have the Greenpeace attack in perspective (e.g., Gattiker, Urs E. June 14, 2010).

When it comes to social media, timing is everything. Moreover, online and offline are two sides of the same coin and cannot be separated. Social media is not another mass broadcast channel and the traditional stonewalling that was used with public relations no longer works with social media. If you do not reply, people just go to the Web and voice their opinions and *the rumor mill may become a huge avalanche of negative publicity.*

Table 5.3 outlines some of the issues that need to be addressed, including having a disaster plan that is tried and tested for that reason. Just because it is Friday after-noon cannot mean that nobody will monitor things until staff gets back on Monday morning or Tuesday after a long weekend. Particularly important is that people know what has to be done and who has to be informed at two o'clock in the morning

Table 5.6 Purpose and value proposition

#	Rating	Improving key drivers and operating metrics such as client satisfaction	Points
5.6.1	*****	Organization's staff has a clear understanding of how using social media relates to the company's key drivers (i.e., employees can succinctly explain what in their area of work is a key driver for helping achieve corporate goals, such as higher profits)	0, 1, 2, or 3
5.6.2	*****	Company measures how social media can help reduce customer returns	…
5.6.3	*****	Organization monitors how social media activities (e.g., purchasing advice, frequently asked questions (FAQs), etc.) help reduce customer complaints	…
5.6.4	*****	Company acknowledges customer endorsements sent via social media channel(s) (e.g., @ComMetrics product arrived, easy to setup—great graphics; My hospital stay at @CareYou was a good experience, knowledgeable staff that knows their stuff. Thanks!)	…
5.6.5	*****	Product feedback is collected systematically and flows into the design of new products and services	…

Note: The total number of points can range from 0 to 3 for each item, which is then multiplied by the number of stars given, ranging from 1 to 5. The range of scores for each item is therefore 0 to 15, which is then multiplied by the number of questions. Accordingly, for the above table, the maximum score is 5 (questions) × 15 = 75

For more information about the calculations, scaling and rationale, please see Table 5.1

as well as the timeframe to be worked with. If negative comments come up on the company's Facebook page, how quickly must administrators reply? Why these comments should not be removed also needs to be discussed. Once agreed upon, this needs to be written down so others will understand why *removal will do more harm than good.*

5.6.2 Purpose and Value Proposition: Link with Key Drivers

Table 5.6 addresses issues very much related to Table 5.1 where we focused on strategy and purpose of social media activities. Most people will agree that *social media is not used to sell product, but to improve customer engagement and/or customer service.* For instance, some argue that 5% higher customer loyalty will increase your profit anywhere from 25% to 85%. However, a dissatisfied customer will let nine other people know about their bad experience, while a satisfied client will only talk to five people about their good experience.

Accordingly, while it is difficult to relate social media to sales, just like your TV commercial, you can connect these activities with key drivers. Examples may include reducing the number of returns, and getting more requests for information via e-mail or the social media comment form.

Table 5.7 Human capital

#	Rating	Human resource management	Points
5.7.1	*****	Have you taken a skills inventory that addresses issues pertaining to which tools and methods staff know well?	0, 1, 2, or 3
5.7.2	*****	Have you taken a skills inventory that addresses issues pertaining to those tools and methods they should know well, but do not yet?	...
5.7.3	*****	Has the company taken an awareness inventory, addressing issues pertaining to how well staff know and understand the opportunities or limitations of using such tools as Facebook, Twitter, and Xing?	...
5.7.4	*****	Has the company taken an awareness inventory addressing issues pertaining to how well staff know and understand the limitations or risks of using such tools as Facebook, Twitter, and Xing?	...
5.7.5	*****	Have training needs been identified for the effective use of certain platforms (e.g., Facebook, Xing, corporate blog, LinkedIn, Tumblr)?	...
5.7.6	*****	Were training needs identified regarding the measurement of results (e.g., employees understand how these are linked to key operators, such as customer complaints)?	...
5.7.7	*****	Were training needs identified regarding the measurement of results (e.g., employees understand how these key operators, such as customer satisfaction, affect strategic measures, such as sales growth)?	...
5.7.8	*****	Have appropriate training programs (e.g., workshops) been identified?	...
5.7.9	*****	Based on work conducted regarding training needs (see Q 5.7.5 to 5.7.7), were employees given the necessary training during the last period?	...
5.7.10	*****	Did you develop a way to monitor the quality of outputs (e.g., monitoring tone or sentiment of responses, brand mentioning's, tweets)?	...
5.7.11	*****	Can your measurement methods show that this process is capable of achieving planned results (see also Q 5.7.3)?	...

Note: The total number of points can range from 0 to 3 for each item, which is then multiplied by the number of stars given, ranging from 1 to 5. The range of scores for each item is therefore 0 to 15, which is then multiplied by the number of questions. Accordingly, for the above table, the maximum score is 11 (questions) × 15 = 165

For more information about the calculations, scaling, and rationale, please see Table 5.1

Table 5.6 raises the questions necessary to ensure that the purpose of your social media use is clearly understood by all staff. In many cases, one of the best uses of social media is to improve the customer experience by providing service, which is a much different focus than trying to reduce costs incured through your call center. Improving the customer experience may not reduce costs, but it does satisfy get your customer's need for information or help fixing a problem faster. In turn, they will likely let others know if your service meets expectations or is remarkably better than your competitor's. There is nothing worse for a client than not getting an answer or having to wait several days for help (Table 5.7).

5.7   Conclusion

In this chapter, the focus was on implementing and maintaining the process, such as your company's Facebook page or corporate blog. Hence, we try to develop it and focus on the inputs and outputs needed to succeed.

For instance, the main ASOS page informs customers about the brand, new trends, and upcoming sales, while ASOSHereToHelp aims to take customer issues off the main Facebook page (see https://www.facebook.com/ASOSHeretoHelp).

ASOS will want to manage the process and the inputs and outputs needed for each of these two pages separately, and the checklists presented here may also be used for each page separately. While this seems feasible for a larger company (i.e., to have two pages or more AND use the forms presented here to manage each process), there is a point of diminishing marginal returns. Of course, it is probably sooner rather than later for a small business. For large organizations, however, I believe using the templates presented here for each page or Twitter account is effective. In other words, there is value in such a systematic analysis. And while the large company may use this approach to analyze the process for each of its Twitter accounts or Facebook pages in every country (e.g., IKEA), a smaller company might have no Twitter account and just one Facebook page, and still be able to use the tools presented here.

Chapter 6 will discuss governance and maintenance of the process.

References

Gattiker, Urs E. (June 14, 2010). ComMetrics weekly review—social media going's on—KitKat vs Greenpeace (see under Tuesday heading). [Blog post—ComMetrics]. Retrieved January 15, 2012, from http://commetrics.com/?p=8802/#

Gattiker, Urs E. (August 25, 2010). Social media's failed acid test: Pakistan disaster response. [Blog post—ComMetrics]. Retrieved January 15, 2012, from http://commetrics.com/?p=9865

Gattiker, Urs E. (April 4, 2011) Can cause marketing damage reputations? [Blog post—ComMetrics]. Retrieved September 8, 2011, from http://commetrics.com/?p=14738

Woo, Gordon (2011) Calculating catastrophe. London, UK. Imperial College

Chapter 6
Governance, Compliance, and Maintenance of the Process

Abstract Chapter 5 focused on managing the process of the social media audit. Chapter 6 puts the spotlight on governance matters and how we can assure that the process is being maintained at a desirable performance level. The focus will be on maintaining quality and consistency, as well as compliance, record keeping and the infrastructure. The human capital available, crisis management process, monitoring and measuring, as well as customer satisfaction are discussed.

In the previous chapter, the focus was on implementing and maintaining the process, such as your company's Facebook page or corporate blog. In this chapter, the focus is on governance and how we can assure that we manage this process properly and maintain oversight and accountability.

Governance is about how companies should be run, in the context of society, the law and best practice. Understanding and managing *governance is an inherent part of the compliance process. Without having the proper governance policies and procedures in place, the company cannot achieve compliance with relevant regulations and laws.*

Governance describes the mechanisms an organization uses to ensure that its constituents follow its established processes and policies. It is the *primary means of maintaining oversight and accountability* in a loosely coupled organizational structure.

A proper governance strategy helps ensure that systems are implemented to monitor and record what is going on, thereby also allowing us to take the necessary steps to ensure compliance with agreed policies. Further, it can provide for corrective action in cases where the rules have been ignored or misconstrued.

Governance provides the structure and processes required for a company to be in compliance with new legislation. To sum up,

1. Governance refers to how an organization controls its actions.
2. Failure to govern may result in not being compliant with regulations and laws, as well as *damage to the company's reputation*, its brand, and loss of customer trust.

3. To tackle this challenge, the company must develop, implement, and administer proper governance strategy, which *must provide for corrective action in cases where the rules have been ignored or misconstrued.*

In this chapter, the focus is on putting into place the controls and procedures for social media activities and tools used for the benefit of the organization and its brand(s). There are numerous examples of how things can go wrong if governance is not implemented according to best practice. For instance, the Forex trades conducted in 2011 by SNB CEO Hildebrand and/or his wife Kashya Hildebrand, a former foreign exchange dealer indicated that not only were the bank's internal guidelines not specific enough to exclude such behavior, the governance needed to enforce those rules was also lacking. This caused a major public relations disaster for the bank and resulted in changes to make the bank's ethical guidelines for its staff and directors more restrictive (see also https://plus.google.com/b/103400392486480 765286/103400392486480765286/posts/YVBtLu1jFTN).

Another example is the Fall 2007 SAS Q400 crash landings. These raised some questions about how Scandinavian Airlines manages its governance regarding maintenance and engineering (for more, see Gattiker, October 29, 2010). A similar example is provided by BP's Deepwater Horizon oil spill in the Gulf of Mexico in 2010 (for more, see Gattiker, Urs E. June 16, 2010).

This illustrates that we must manage the process in an orderly fashion, not only to show that we document what we do but, most importantly, we control our actions to manage risks more effectively. This is outlined in more detail below.

6.1 Managing and Organizing the Process

In the context of social media, the process needs to be managed as outlined in Table 6.1. For instance, it is better to have several people and functions involved than just one or two people from the same department. Similarly, content from various people representing different functions is more interesting to your audience than if it all comes from one person. The exception might be the CEO's blog or Twitter account, where people want to read only a single voice. Of course, having somebody blog or tweet for the CEO is not a wise choice, since eventually it will become public knowledge, and does not help build trust either.

As Table 6.1 suggests, people need to be given the time necessary to do whatever they must with social media on behalf of the company (e.g., replying to customer requests). Here, the critical thing is that people are likely to underestimate time, as numerous surveys have shown regarding people's time spent commuting to and from work, watching TV, doing e-mail, and using Facebook for private purposes, to name a few.

Remember when you thought it took 5 minutes to upgrade a software package or download and install Windows Security Updates? It often tends to be a few minutes more than we thought. Similarly, we need to carefully assess if the resources

Table 6.1 Management and organization

#	Rating	Questions for quality assurance	Points
6.1.1	*****	Does middle management routinely report to top management on the status and effectiveness of social media activities?	0, 1, 2, or 3
6.1.2	*****	Was a process owner (who is responsible for what, when, and how) appointed?	…
	*****	Was there more than one person assigned to work with social media (e.g., using tools and updating blog)?	…
6.1.2	*****	Are the people involved with social media activities on behalf of the company representing various functions (e.g., corporate communications, human resources, marketing, and accounting)?	…
6.1.4	*****	Is responsibility for new content (e.g., blog, white papers, Facebook updates) assigned to and shared between several people?	…
6.1.5	*****	Is responsibility for new content (e.g., blog, white papers, Facebook updates) assigned to and shared between several functions (e.g., marketing, R&D and human resources)?	…
6.1.6	*****	Does the team (or staff member) have the resources needed to implement and manage this process?	…
6.1.7	*****	Does the team (or staff member) have the resources (e.g., manpower, time at work) needed to tweet on Twitter and/or share on Facebook?	…
6.1.8	*****	Does the team (or staff member) have the resources (e.g., manpower, time at work) needed to research and write the blog posts planned (e.g., release one every 2 weeks)?	…
6.1.9	*****	Do team members have time to reply to reader comments left on the corporate blog or Facebook?	…

Note: The total number of points can range from 0 to 3 for each item, which is then multiplied by the number of stars given, ranging from 1 to 5. The range of scores for each item is therefore 0 to 15, which is then multiplied by the number of questions. Accordingly, for the above table, the maximum score is 9 (questions) × 15 = 135

For more information about the calculations, scaling, and rationale, please see Table 5.1

and manpower available are enough to accomplish what we want. If not, we have to note this and management can then either provide more or find other ways, such as lowering targets and expectations, to allow satisfactory performance within the means provided.

6.2 Human Capital

We have to make sure that staff really do have the skills we think are required to handle social media smartly. For instance, there have been cases where people lost their job after the company objected to their LinkedIn profile—specifically that they checked off the box indicating they were interested in career opportunities.

Table 6.2 Human capital: Skill set

#	Rating	Questions	Points
6.2.1	*****	Do you give new employees the opportunity to acquire the skills needed to use social media effectively (e.g., according to guidelines)?	0, 1, 2, or 3
6.2.2	*****	Did your staff upgrade their skills to formulate tweets correctly (retweet, reply, content, language, etc.)?	...
6.2.3	*****	Did staff get the training needed to be able to respond to positive AND negative blog comments (e.g., type of language used)?	...
6.2.4	*****	Did employees get training in how to respond to a crisis unfolding on social media channels (e.g., Facebook—group of users attacking your brand)?	...
6.2.5	*****	Do you discuss with staff what inappropriate behavior consists of regarding language, tweets, Facebook updates, and so forth, using examples and cases to make your point?	...
6.2.6	*****	With social media, there are no right or wrong actions—just choices and consequences. Do your employees understand what could embarrass them and what might get them into trouble or fired (e.g., what if your LinkedIn or Xing profile solicits jobs—see also http://mem.to/t/g/17tami225)?	...

Note: The total number of points can range from 0 to 3 for each item, which is then multiplied by the number of stars given, ranging from 1 to 5. The range of scores for each item is therefore 0 to 15, which is then multiplied by the number of questions. Accordingly, for the above table, the maximum score is 6 (questions) × 15 = 90

For more information about the calculations, scaling, and rationale, please see Table 5.1

This is an example of how the rules of the socially networked world do not always mesh comfortably with the world of work. In the world of social media, there are no right or wrong actions—just choices and consequences.

However, to survive this jungle employees need help acquiring the skills required to navigate this maze of ever changing rules and role models. The questions in Table 6.2 address this to some extent and help you take inventory and assess if staff have the skill set needed to succeed with using social media.

6.3   Infrastructure

Adopting innovations and new ways for engaging with clients also requires that the necessary technology be put in place. Table 6.3 outlines some of the issues that need to be addressed.

One problem that may arise is that part-time staff or those from your outsourcer may use different tools and technologies than you do. Another could be that people do not have the license to use certain tools on their private PC or smartphone. And even if they do, using their personal hardware for things like chatting online with clients, are the chat logs archived?

Table 6.3 Infrastructure: Technology, tools, and software

#	Rating	Questions	Points
6.3.1	*****	Does the company have the software this process requires?	0, 1, 2, or 3
6.3.2	*****	Are support services in place for this service (e.g., who to ask if things are unclear)?	…
6.3.2	*****	Are data retention services in place as required by law (e.g., backup of chat and tweets)?	…
6.3.4	*****	Do employees have the necessary hardware needed to engage using social media (e.g., tweet or reply to a blog comment) outside the workplace (e.g., mobile Internet access or broadband connection from home)?	…
6.3.5	*****	Can employees use the software tools required to engage using social media (e.g., tweet or reply to a blog comment) outside the workplace (e.g., mobile Internet access or broadband connection from home)?	…
6.3.6	*****	Have copyright issues been addressed regarding using software the company has a license for with private equipment (e.g., PC at home or with private smartphone)?	…
6.3.7	*****	Has information security been addressed regarding replying to blog comments or accessing data files when using private equipment (e.g., virtual private network is being used to login to manage the blog's dashboard)?	…

Note: The total number of points can range from 0 to 3 for each item, which is then multiplied by the number of stars given, ranging from 1 to 5. The range of scores for each item is therefore 0 to 15, which is then multiplied by the number of questions. Accordingly, for the above table, the maximum score is 7 (questions) × 15 = 105

For more information about the calculations, scaling, and rationale, please see Table 5.1

For instance, using Google Talk allows one to keep all conversations and have Google send a full transcript of the chat as an e-mail. However, the company also needs a copy of those e-mails and/or access to the account to archive such conversations.

Table 6.3 poses some of the questions that must be asked and discussed in your company to ensure these issues are addressed satisfactorily. If the infrastructure, tools, and software are not up to par, this may later come back to haunt the company.

Electronic discovery (also called e-discovery or ediscovery) is the *obligation of parties to a lawsuit to exchange documents that exist only in electronic form* (known as ESI or electronically stored information). Organizations must preserve and be able to produce electronic evidence. *Examples of electronic documents and data subject to e-discovery include e-mails, voicemails, instant or chat messages, e-calendars, audio files, data on handheld devices, animation, metadata, graphics, photographs, videos, spreadsheets, Web sites, drawings, and other types of digital data.*

6.4 Governance and Compliance

As discussed in the previous section, archiving in case of e-discovery has become an increasingly critical activity. Accordingly, technology and software have to be put in place to be able to produce electronically stored information if asked by a judge or a government agency. In addition to the technology angle, e-discovery also requires that our procedures be such that relevant information and records are archived.

The importance of these issues for compliance, e-discovery, etc. has been illustrated in numerous cases. For instance, key e-mails were produced that ultimately led former chair of the Swiss National Back Philipp Hildebrand to step down from his post on January 9, 2012 (see here http://mem.to/t/g/52qbmi979). In 2011, Christian Wulff—Germany's president—was faced with an archived voicemail and a transcript that suggested he had threatened a journalist from the tabloid *Bild*. In particular, he wanted the newspaper not to go public with certain information about his house purchase a few years back.

By addressing such issues with the help of the questions raised in Table 6.4, you should be in a position to structure this work by using the template in Table 6.4 and systematically applying it to the organizational context you are supposed

Table 6.4 Compliance and record keeping

#	Rating	Questions	Points
6.4.1	*****	Did you establish the records needed for monitoring process inputs?	0, 1, 2, or 3
6.4.2	*****	Did you establish the records needed for monitoring outputs?	...
6.4.3	*****	Did you establish the records needed to control the process inputs?	...
6.4.4	*****	Did you establish the records needed to control the process outputs?	...
6.4.5	*****	Are the records enabling you to demonstrate that this process meets regulatory requirements created?	...
6.4.6	*****	Are the process outputs legally compliant (e.g., data protection and insider trading)?	...
6.4.7	*****	Have you established tried and tested procedures for controlling the quality of process inputs (e.g., white papers, other people's blog posts—see http://commetrics.com/?p=16230)?	...
6.4.8	*****	Is the process used to check quality of output (i.e., before tweeting) compliant with legal requirements?	...
6.4.9	*****	Does the process used to check quality of output (i.e., before tweeting) represent proper due diligence?	...

Note: The total number of points can range from 0 to 3 for each item, which is then multiplied by the number of stars given, ranging from 1 to 5. The range of scores for each item is therefore 0 to 15, which is then multiplied by the number of questions. Accordingly, for the above table, the maximum score is 8 (questions) × 15 = 135

For more information about the calculations, scaling, and rationale, please see Table 5.1

to audit. Whether the right procedures have been put in place to minimize or at least successfully manage the inherent risks will also be revealed.

Record keeping and being ready for e-discovery is also a question of risk management. Put differently, *you may be within the law, but unable to produce the required voicemail, blog comment, discussion group entry, or wall post left on the company's page.*

If nothing else, you need to be aware of how to proceed if you have to ask the operator or owner of the platform, such as LinkedIn, to help you produce a document asked for by the court. For instance, you may be required to turn over your computer archives in response to the defendant's e-discovery requests. Table 6.4 should help to systemize these procedures and show management where improvements are needed (Gattiker, not dated).

6.5 Maintaining Quality

Making sure that the quality of tweets can be maintained is a real challenge, but it is vital that Twitter replies to customers maintain consistent excellence. Being polite and staying on topic regardless of how irate the customer might be comes to mind here.

Issues outlined in Table 6.5 also relate to Table 6.2, since we need to make sure that staff have the skills needed to cope with these challenges successfully. For instance, using a tool such as twitterfeed may not be acceptable according your quality standards. To explain, once registered as a user, twitterfeed allows you to register a blog's RSS feed. In turn, the program will visit the site of the RSS feed after 1 or 24 hours depending upon your chosen preference. When the blog publishes new content, twitterfeed then picks it up and tweets it for you.

Quite a few people publish content from BBC, Mashable, or Huffington Post on their Twitter account using twitterfeed or other tools. Unfortunately, this does not allow one to follow the necessary quality procedure, which requires that you first read the content from A to Z to satisfy yourself that the article meets your standard for quality and appropriateness. Only then can you craft a tweet and send it out.

A similar example is Tumblr. This social network allows one to have a personal blog. Most often, blog posts are rather short, word-wise, but include images and may link to a video or other blog posts. Similarly, Paper.li and tag-allow people to use your tweet to create their own type of electronic daily to share with others. However, your clients may appreciate if you link to the original story, saving them one or two clicks and having to glance through the summary provided. *Allow your target audience to get where they always wanted to go—the original content—quicker.* Yes, this means you need to recheck and spend time yourself before you can be sure the content is what you are after. Of course, this is what

Table 6.5 Maintaining quality and consistency

#	Rating	Questions	Points
6.5.1	*****	Do employees know how to write a great Facebook wall post versus Facebook note, poll, or discussion item (e.g., defined with the help of examples)?	0, 1, 2, or 3
6.5.2	*****	Do employees know how to write a great blog post and/or blog comment (i.e., company has defined this with an example or two)?	...
6.5.3	*****	If an employee is responding on behalf of the company to a client tweet, blog post, comment, or in a discussion threat on another platform (e.g., LinkedIn or Xing group), did they receive hands-on training on how to reply properly when trying to point out an inaccurate representation of facts about the brand or organization on these platforms?	...
6.5.4	*****	Did staff get training on how to properly reply to an angry client comment or request on the blog or discussion forum on the company Web site?	...
6.5.5	*****	Do your social media activities reflect your desire to encourage more engagement with your audience when they are online by releasing new content regularly on the days your target group is most likely to see the material and therefore engage (e.g., a new blog post every second on Sunday around 1:00 am GMT is not helpful)?	...
6.5.6	*****	Do your social media activities reflect your desire to encourage more engagement with your audience when they are online by releasing new content regularly on the days your target group is most likely to see the material and therefore engage (e.g., 1 tweet at 7:00 am and/or 12:00 noon and/or 5:00 pm GMT on workdays)?	...
6.5.7	*****	Do your social media activities reflect your desire to encourage more engagement with your audience when they are online by releasing new content regularly on the days your target group is most likely to see the material and therefore engage (e.g., posting twice a week on Google+ or Facebook around the same time, such as every Thursday and Sunday?	...
6.5.8	*****	Is posting across social media platforms divided up appropriately among staff to assure consistency during the work week?	...
6.5.9	*****	Is posting across social media platforms divided up appropriately among staff to assure consistency on public holidays and weekends?	...
6.5.10	*****	Do employees understand that before they retweet something they need to make sure they link to the original source (e.g., the university where one can download the research paper)? Retweeting without checking beforehand may result in your followers ending up on another site that says two things about the paper, misrepresents the result or uses foul language. Checking before reposting anything including tweets is a must.	...
6.5.11	*****	Does your staff understand the ropes to skip or netiquette for Twitter, Facebook, and so forth?	

Note: Some of the above, such as who posts when on the weekends, must be written down in a manual. Some training is needed to enable staff to perform well (e.g., 6.5.1 and 6.5.10). Discussing examples during team meetings on how to do it right versus wrong is needed here

The total number of points can range from 0 to 3 for each item, which is then multiplied by the number of stars given, ranging from 1 to 5. The range of scores for each item is therefore 0 to 15, which is then multiplied by the number of questions. Accordingly, for the above table, the maximum score is 11 (questions) × 15 = 165

For more information about the calculations, scaling, and rationale, please see Table 5.1

your clients and followers expect from you and deserve, considering the trust they put in content you share.

Accordingly, quality is also a way to ensure that you *do not waste your reader's or follower's attention while you have it* by requiring them to jump through too many hoops. Plent of data suggests that many people leave a Web page or do not click the links to get to the original source if more than 5 seconds are wasted this way (see also Table 6.5).

Managing quality also means that your staff understand that Facebook content is not the same as Twitter content. Posting the same tweet on Facebook and Twitter might be possible (e.g., by using Ping.fm or Tweetdeck), but it might not be the smartest way to engage with clients. In short, those on Facebook are very likely looking for different types of content (e.g., from family and friends, fund and images) than those following you on Twitter (i.e., news).

The above illustrates that there must be *a deeper understanding of what purpose the company wants to pursue using various social networks* (e.g., using Facebook, Google+) *and its Web site and/or blog*. Additionally, we must assess whether staff have the skills required to handle the job smartly and carefully manage the risks involved. Without some training, whether in-house or elsewhere, including discussions during team meetings with examples illustrating the good, bad, or ugly, do not expect things to go smoothly.

6.6 Crisis Management

Everyone has heard about cases where the use of social media may have exacerbated a public relations nightmare experienced by a company. Examples include Néstlé's KitKat brand being attacked with a Greenpeace video that went viral (see http://commetrics.com/?p=7607 under point 5) or BP and the Deepwater Horizon oil spill in the Gulf of Mexico (see http://commetrics.com/?p=8359). These and many more are examples of companies that have experienced damage to their reputation or brand due to customers discussing their behavior on social media channels.

For any crisis you need to have a plan or disaster management checklist that spells out what has to be done. Ideally, it is short, and like the fire drill, it has been tried and tested to see if it works. The questions listed in Table 6.6 are a good beginning for getting this process started (Gattiker, August 11, 2010).

The list in Table 6.6 also illustrates why it is important that employees are aware of these procedures and know what to do in case of an evolving disaster and crisis. Often staff are unsure what to do and how to behave in case of such an occurrence. If people do not know what to do in an emergency, valuable time is lost and the patient may die. The same applies when a possible public relations disaster is in the making. Competent and timely responses are absolutely required.

Table 6.6 Contingency planning and crisis management

#	Rating	Questions	Points
6.6.1	*****	Have *systemic risks* (e.g., cloud service is down, unable to access content) been identified and their potential impact (e.g., services unavailable) and costs (e.g., annoyed customers, lost sales) assessed?	0, 1, 2, or 3
6.6.2	*****	Have *non-systemic risks* (e.g., activist group has launched an online campaign against your brand) been identified and their potential impact (e.g., bad press) and costs (e.g., annoyed customers, lost sales) assessed?	...
6.6.3	*****	Has the organization prioritized three major risks (systemic and/or non-systemic ones), while also *calculating opportunity costs* in the event that such a highly possible event does actually occur?	...
6.6.4	*****	Have you established a system (e.g., process to help you determine who monitors what) that allows you to monitor for the above prioritized risks on social media channels during public holidays, weekends, and vacation periods?	...
6.6.5	*****	Have you put in place a contingency plan that spells out response mechanisms? For instance, if case A happens (e.g., based on potential seriousness and probability of occurrence), staff members Y and Z will do as follows (e.g., who has to be informed, who speaks for the company to the media, and who replies online) within X hours	
6.6.6	*****	To help prevent a *possible public relations disaster*, *has the above contingency plan been tested* to see if the procedures put in place work well in case of such a risk materializing (e.g., group launches attack against company on Facebook or Google+)?	...
6.6.7	*****	During the last 12 months, has the above *contingency plan been tested with a random fire drill during a holiday or long weekend?* A long weekend might happen if Thursday is a public holiday and many workers bridge Friday by taking a vacation day or compensating time off to get a 4-day weekend. A great time to launch an attack against a brand is the afternoon of the day before a long weekend.	...

Note: Total score can range from 0 to 3 for each item, which is then multiplied by the number of stars given, ranging from 1 to 5. The range of scores for each item is therefore 0 to 15, which is then multiplied by the number of questions. Accordingly, for the above table, the maximum score is 7 (questions) × 15 = 105

For more information about the calculations, scaling, and rationale, please see Table 5.1

6.7 Customer Satisfaction

Table 5.7 made a start by pointing out that key drivers are likely to involve customer-related issues, such as social media helping to reduce customer complaints or resolving such issues quicker.

This section (see Table 6.7) is mainly about how we can make sure that what we tweet, publish on our Facebook wall, write about on our blog, or offer in white

Table 6.7 Customer satisfaction

#	Rating	Ensuring what we offer meets client needs	Points
6.7.1	*****	Do you measure how satisfied your readers are with your blog content (e.g., 3-question customer survey-online or offline)?	0, 1, 2, or 3
6.7.2	*****	Have you asked your Twitter followers what they like about your tweets and what they find not so helpful?	...
6.7.3	*****	Have you asked your Facebook fans what they like about your wall posts, and what is less useful?	...
6.7.4	*****	Have you asked your followers (fill in the name of the platform, such as Google+) or group members (e.g., on LinkedIn and Xing) which content they like the most and why, and those they find less useful?	...
6.7.5	*****	Can you demonstrate how social customer relationship management activities (sCRM) create synergies, such as increasing how many customer inquiries can be resolved online versus on the phone or by visiting the customer (using absolute numbers and/or percentages)?	...
6.7.6	*****	Have you asked key customers about what kind of content they would value coming from you (i.e., helps them in their jobs) with a short survey, either online or offline?	...

Note: The total number of points can range from 0 to 3 for each item, which is then multiplied by the number of stars given, ranging from 1 to 5. The range of scores for each item is therefore 0 to 15, which is then multiplied by the number of questions. Accordingly, for the above table, the maximum score is 6 (questions) × 15 = 90

For more information about the calculations, scaling, and rationale, please see Table 5.1

papers for download fulfills the client's desire. Unless the material is of interest to customers and helps them do their jobs better, one must ask if the activity serves any purpose that helps your company's bottom line. *A charity will not want to share images, testimonials or stories about events, if neither volunteers nor donors care about such content.*

When we implement a process, we often need to go back and ask how we are doing. We also must *make sure that we do not just hear those that shout the loudest.* In fact, it is just as important to get feedback from those who are quiet (sometimes called the silent majority). Accordingly, we need formal and less formal ways to follow up with our clients. This might be an exit survey on the Web site that randomly asks every 100th visitor as they leave the site 3–5 short questions. For example, did they find the information or content they came looking for?

Or we might send an e-mail to every person that unsubscribes from our e-mail blog post subscription service. Often, the feedback might be that they changed jobs and needed to use another address. However, sometimes it might be our content that gets them to unsubscribe. Fortunately, people are generally quite willing to share if asked politely the reasons why they unsubscribe or no longer want or need our content. Such information has to be used to assess if we are still on target by providing content that our clients and target audience value.

6.8 Purpose and Value Proposition: Measurement

The number of engagement activities, clicks, inbound links, and subscribers gained is often used for measurement. Unfortunately, as long as we keep it limited to these simple numbers or how many people signed up, people will be driven to waste time trying to increase those types of measures.

Nevertheless, metrics must also include measures that address how active or engaged people are (e.g., see Chapter 2, Table 2.3). Only then can we generate more sensible objectives or targets for our work with social media. Such measures will then also facilitate our efforts to move people through the sales funnel by building the trust required to engage in business relationships.

Table 6.8 addresses some of these issues. In particular, it focuses on getting staff ready to monitor social media activities that can be linked to key drivers. For instance, if top management wishes to increase sales next year showing *social media's link to that key driver will be important*.

Table 6.8 Monitoring and measuring

#	Rating	Purpose and value proposition	Points
6.8.1	*****	Do employees know how to monitor social media channels with which tools?	0, 1, 2, or 3
6.8.2	*****	Do your employees know how to monitor for which keywords?	…
6.8.3	*****	Do your employees know which tools to use to get a feeling regarding sentiment about your brand or company?	…
6.8.4	*****	Does staff know what their monitoring duties are, such as who monitors the brand's the Facebook page or Twitter replies during working hours (e.g., how often between 7:00 am and 8:00 pm)?	…
6.8.5	*****	Does staff know what their monitoring duties are, such as who monitors your Facebook page or Twitter replies during public holidays and weekends?	…
6.8.6	*****	Do process personnel know which data will be collected to get what kind of key metrics (e.g., unique page visitors and time needed to respond to customer inquiries on corporate blog)?	…
6.8.7	*****	Do employees understand how customer satisfaction statistics/data will be collected to assess the effectiveness of process output?	…
6.8.8	*****	Do you have a formalized procedure in place measuring sentiment on such channels as Twitter, Facebook, blog, etc.?	…

Note: Please remember, when asked about a feature clients often express interest, but when the feature or content is offered, will they really use—READ—your blog content? If content is critical to do their job better, it is more likely to be consumed

Total score can range from 0 to 3 for each item, which is then multiplied by the number of stars given, ranging from 1 to 5. The range of scores for each item is therefore 0 to 15, which is then multiplied by the number of questions. Accordingly, for the above table, the maximum score is 8 (questions) × 15 = 120

For more information about the calculations, scaling, and rationale, please see Table 5.1

Employees also need to understand how these things will be measured as far as output and quality is concerned. To illustrate, employee goals should be assessed and discussed during performance appraisals. Similarly, employees need to know how their social media performance will be measured. Table 6.8 lists some questions that help you better address this matter within your organization.

6.9   Conclusion

In this chapter, the focus was on addressing governance, compliance, and the maintenance process for our social media activities. A particular focus was put on how we manage the process and if the skill set our employees have is appropriate. To illustrate, if a visitor needs to print something from a USB stick, employees need to know if they have a USB port and what to do to ensure no malicious code or files inadvertently infect their system. In *most instances, the company has an established procedure, but the challenge is to make sure that employees know about it and can easily follow it.* The same applies to social media challenges and what e-discovery means for each employee. Unless they understand and can easily conform to the rules, nonconformities are likely to occur frequently.

Another concern is that, in order to maintain our process while continuing to achieve quality results, certain things need to be understood. Accordingly, our Facebook fan may not appreciate the same type of content as our blog reader (e.g., white paper, checklist). Instead, they may prefer images, short comments or notes, and so on automatically retweeting links and stories or posting them on our Facebook page is also not the kind of quality assurance we are striving for.

Besides maintaining consistency, Chapter 6 also outlined how we can address contingency planning and crisis management. Customer satisfaction regarding social media participation and content was discussed as well.

Chapter 7 will move to quality assurance and control. We address how a well maintained process' outputs need to be evaluated to ensure they meet the quality standard(s) we have set for ourselves.

References

Gattiker, Urs E. (Not dated). Governance. [Blog page – info.CyTRAP.eu]. Retrieved January 19, 2012, from http://info.cytrap.eu//?page_id=59

Gattiker, Urs, E. (June 16, 2010). How BP shrugs off negative reviews. [Blog post – ComMetrics]. Retrieved February 13, 2012, from http://commetrics.com/?p=8359

Gattiker, Urs E. (August 11, 2010). Social media DO's and DON'Ts: 6 remedies for any emergency. [Blog post – ComMetrics]. Retrieved January 19, 2012, from http://commetrics.com/?p=9456

Gattiker, Urs, E. (October 29, 2010). SAS risk management – after 2 crashes we expected proper risk assessment but got another crash-landing instead (UPDATE 1). [Blog post – info.CyTRAP.eu]. Retrieved January 31, 2012, from http://info.cytrap.eu//?p=119

Chapter 7
Evaluating the Process: Quality Assurance

Abstract Firms sometimes run social media marketing by the seat of their pants, *lacking clear direction or established goals.* This kind of chaotic adoption provides little control or quality assurance. This chapter focuses *on limiting the proliferation risk,* while streamlining the process management. We present *tools for improving quality control and assurance* to *achieve a unified brand image.*

In Chapter 6, the focus was on implementing and maintaining the process, such as your company's Facebook page or corporate blog, as well as examining and evaluating this process. Chapter 7 focuses on quality assurance of the process, such as what will be evaluated regarding the quality of our Facebook page process, as well as how deep and thorough the scope of this evaluation should be. Once again, templates in the form of tables are provided to help you conduct this work in your organization. Please adjust them to fit your context; in other words, delete or remove what might not be necessary and expand and go into more detail where necessary to assess your organization's unique situation.

At the lowest level, evaluation is a regular social activity, such as when we evaluate *how much we enjoy our lunch* special. Here, we make comparisons amongst products or services we may have experienced in the past. Sometimes, we also *evaluate to decide to purchase one brand over another.* Of course, the criteria used are not the same for everyone evaluating. For instance, for some the cost of a car or dinner may outweigh all other criteria in the choice process. In social media, the purposes and criteria are inevitably more complex. Evaluation is the process of acquiring information that can, and often does, raise a series of difficult and sometimes contentious issues. Some of the concerns we need to raise include:

1. Who wants the evaluation (e.g., top management, marketing, and/or sales)?
2. What do they need to know?
3. Why do they want to know (e.g., is it for budgetary decision-making)?
4. What will they do with the information (e.g., positive brand mentions drop or increase, what will they do to change the number for the next quarter)?

Once the above have been answered, it might be advisable to address the following questions before embarking on any evaluation:

1. What processes or outputs depend on the outcomes and findings?
2. Will the outcome affect financial and human resources or could it result in redundancies?
3. What is the salient issue for the evaluation (e.g., changing our approach, closing local Facebook pages, or posting more on Twitter or our corporate blog)?
4. Whose opinion regarding quality assurance counts most (e.g., customers, management, or suppliers)?

As the above illustrates, *evaluation of social media activities in companies encompasses competing criteria and purposes*. The evaluation of a company's social media activities involves *making judgments about the worth* and effectiveness of organizational intentions, processes and outcomes. It is situated in potentially sensitive *operational, economic, and ethical contexts*.

Evaluating social media activities means the systematic collection of data and sifting through it, as well as making judgments about the validity of information (i.e., does it measure what it is supposed to?) and inferences we derive from these data. Finally, *evaluation involves our judgment about whether the results attained warrant if the efforts and resources invested*.

How we collect and interpret data is influenced by the factors outlined above. Most important is that we do not make judgments that are influenced by our values, beliefs, etc. Accordingly, evaluation findings must be discussed and documented, in order to sway friends and foes.

When we talk about *defining the scope of evaluating the process*, in this case social media activities undertaken by the firm, we are talking about *developing a common understanding as to what is included in, or excluded from, the evaluation.* In short, what are the boundaries of the project?

By contrast, *when we talk about focus*, we need to decide what issues and challenges we want to learn more about. Is it micro-blogging on Twitter or blogging on a corporate blog? of course, both are different processes where different content is shared in vastly different ways. *The focus of a social media evaluation is on processes and not a person or product.* A process audit of social media *examines the effectiveness of company procedures.*

7.1 Scope of the Evaluation

Table 7.1 addresses the issue of scope. With the help of these questions, we can *determine what the quality audit and evaluation might include and what might not be included.* In the context here, scope means how extensive the audit will be or *how much into detail we need to go.*

Table 7.1 Scope of the evaluation

#	Rating	Questions pertaining to the scope of the quality assurance audit component—are we effective in how we do things?	Points
7.1.1	*****	Can we collect information effectively regarding mentioning of our brand on such as Twitter, Facebook, or Google Plus?	0, 1, 2, or 3
7.1.2	*****	Based on 7.1.1, do we know how to effectively interpret the monitoring information (e.g., mentions are…. positive, and negative)?	
7.1.3	*****	The audit evaluates what is being done with the data collected (e.g., see 7.1.1 and 7.1.2), e.g., if so many mentions are positive what actions are taken?	…
7.1.4	*****	The audit does address the effectiveness of the employees' know-how about how to monitor social media channels with tools we use	
7.1.5	*****	The audit does evaluate the effectiveness of the human resource skills upgrading efforts undertaken during the period reviewed and/or the attained competence levels achieved by staff	…
7.1.6	*****	The audit evaluates the suitability of infrastructure	…
7.1.7	*****	The audit evaluates the suitability of tools and software	…
7.1.8	*****	The audit evaluates the effectiveness of the maintenance of the social media service	…
7.1.9	*****	The audit evaluates the effectiveness of the monitoring methods. For instance, how do we know and do we need to know when somebody mentions our brand on Twitter, Facebook, or Google Plus?	
7.1.10	*****	The audit evaluates the effectiveness of the measurement methods	
7.1.11	*****	The audit evaluates the effectiveness of the process inputs including their quality	…

Note: Depending upon the scope of the audit (how much depth is required?), breath (how wide will our net be?) and depth (how much detail is there needed?) we require (see also Table 4.1), some of the questions posed above may not apply. For instance, systematically monitoring mentions across the Web for a small company with less than 100 employees may not be an effective and smart way to use resources. The story may differ for a Fortune 500 firm

The total number of points can range from 0 to 3 for each item, which is then multiplied by the number of stars given, ranging from 1 to 5. The range of scores for each item is therefore 0 to 15, which is then multiplied by the number of questions. Accordingly, for the above table, the maximum score is 11 (questions) × 15 = 165

For more information about the calculations, scaling, and rationale, please see Table 5.1

Accordingly, a medium-sized company with less than 500 employees will perform a less extensive and complex audit than what might be needed for a global corporation. The latter's divisions and country subsidiaries might each warrant an audit encompassing the full scope of the evaluation.

Table 7.1 outlines the questions that could be asked including but not limited to such things as if the software or hardware are suitable for the tasks we have given ourselves using social media.

7.2 Focus of the Evaluation

Table 7.2 addresses the focus of the evaluation. In the context of the audit process, we are interested in determining which parts of the social media process should be evaluated further. We could look at one process such as sharing internal research with the outside using social media. In contrast, we may have to duplicate Table 7.2 because we want to also evaluate how well we do regarding our research on various platforms such as slideshare.com, Scribd.com, or papers.com

Here, we are interested to assess if we achieved the planned results as set with objectives and performance targets in such wide-ranging areas as measurement, monitoring, process input, and so forth as listed in Table 7.2. It also focuses the beam on the issue of customer engagement that is not easy to define but must to enable us to address if we reached our performance targets (Gattiker, Urs E. March 14 2011).

Table 7.2 Focus of evaluation

#	Rating	Questions pertaining to the focus of the evaluation for one or more processes or a combination thereof	Points
7.2.1	*****	Is the process (i.e., social media marketing) achieving the planned results in monitoring?	0, 1, 2, or 3
7.2.2	*****	Is the process (i.e., social media marketing) achieving the planned results in measurement?	…
7.2.3	*****	Is the process (i.e., social media marketing) achieving the planned results in output feedback?	…
7.2.4	*****	Is the process (i.e., social media marketing) achieving the planned results in customer feedback (for instance, how well does our e-mail newsletter meet customer requirements)?	…
7.2.5	*****	Is the process (i.e., social media marketing) achieving the planned results regarding record keeping activities (to facilitate governance and compliance efforts)?	…
7.2.6	*****	Is the process (i.e., social media marketing) achieving the planned results in customer engagement (e.g., blog comments, request for quotes and people talking about us online)?	…
7.2.7	*****	Is the process (i.e., social media marketing) being hindered in achieving the planned results due to inadequate infrastructure, tools and/or software?	…
7.2.8	*****	Is the process owner or manager of social media marketing activities achieving an acceptable level of competence?	…

Note: Depending upon the scope (how much depth is required?), breadth (how wide will our net be?) and depth (how much detail is needed?) we require (see also Table 4.1) of the audit, some of the questions posed above may not apply. For instance, systematically monitoring mentions across the Web for a small company with less than 100 employees may not be an effective and smart way to use resources. The story may differ for a Fortune 500 firm

The total number of points can range from 0 to 3 for each item, which is then multiplied by the number of stars given, ranging from 1 to 5. The range of scores for each item is therefore 0 to 15, which is then multiplied by the number of questions. Accordingly, for the above table, the maximum score is 8 (questions) × 15 = 120

For more information about the calculations, scaling, and rationale, please see Table 5.1

It is advisable to discuss these focus issues more thoroughly by canvassing various stakeholder groups such as clients and suppliers as well as employees. Some of these should then also be made part of the group after the audit has been completed, when findings will be discussed and analyzed and suggestions for improvement will be made.

Of course, if questions 7.2.1 up to including 7.2.7 have never been discussed so far, it will be difficult to find much during an audit. The issue here is also that before you embark on the audit the questions outlined in Table 7.2 are discussed and if necessary an objective/target is set against which we intend to benchmark ourselves.

7.3 Methods of Evaluation

Table 7.3 addresses the methods we use to evaluate our social media marketing activities. The purpose is to evaluate how certain things have been implemented. For instance, is the implementation of the Facebook page following best practice, including the regulatory requirements that require disclosing who is behind a page in Europe (e.g., company's legal address, phone number, etc.)?

Table 7.3 Methods of evaluation—how we go about it

#	Rating	Questions	Points
7.3.1	*****	Do you conduct regular audits (i.e., systematically review the process and performance) of social media marketing activities?	0, 1, 2, or 3
7.3.2	*****	Do you conduct regular audits (i.e., systematically review the process and performance) of how well certain social media marketing activities have been implemented (e.g., when answering customer inquiries on a special Facebook or Google+ page)?	...
7.3.3	*****	Does the organization assess how well certain social media marketing processes work (e.g., answering incoming request for help via e-mail, Twitter, or blog post)?	...
7.3.4	*****	Does the company evaluate if certain social media marketing activities meet set performance targets?	...
7.3.5	*****	Do management reviews of social media marketing activities (or specific processes therein) compare audit data with the previous period (see also point 7.8.1)?	...
7.3.6	*****	Do management reviews of social media marketing activities discuss customer feedback (i.e., input from clients using the output of this process—e.g., subscribers to the newsletter)?	...
7.3.7	*****	Do management reviews of social media marketing activities evaluate customer requirements for this output process (e.g., content of newsletter, Facebook page that clients need the most—relevancy for them)?	...

(continued)

Table 7.3 (continued)

#	Rating	Questions	Points
7.3.8	*****	Do management reviews of social media marketing activities discuss regulatory process requirements (do we meet them)?	...
7.4.9	*****	Do management reviews of social media marketing activities focus on how a process can be improved to exploit opportunities more effectively?	

Note: Please remember that the above set of questions can be used for each single social media marketing activity, such as answering customer inquiries, suggestions, cries for help on a special Facebook page, as well as each separate Twitter account or blog. Put differently, you may choose to use the above list to get an overall assessment or a detailed one for each different part of your social media marketing activities

The total number of points can range from 0 to 3 for each item, which is then multiplied by the number of stars given, ranging from 1 to 5. The range of scores for each item is therefore 0 to 15, which is then multiplied by the number of questions. Accordingly, for the above table, the maximum score is 9 (questions) × 15 = 135

For more information about the calculations, scaling, and rationale, please see Table 5.1

As Table 7.3 suggests, we have to systematically review the process and how well certain social media marketing activities work. For instance, if we start an online campaign to get families to sign up online to join a new virtual community with their customer loyalty number, as Migros did in early 2012, it must be easy to do. Moreover, if it fails to work and people answer with a tweet asking for help, a brush off answer telling the client to call the customer hotline (a toll number with a long wait for an agent) might not be the thing to do (Gattiker, Urs E. not dated, Gattiker, Urs E. February 12, 2012). Some organizations have been a bit more successful doing this than others (Gattiker, Urs E. October 6, 2011).

In the above examples, the evaluation would try to assess if the way the company handles these issues is the best way to do it, both considering the amount of resources required and getting the client's problem resolved satisfactorily and quickly. Table 7.3 provides a template for the questions that need addressing and help one go through this process step by step.

7.4 Customer Satisfaction

Customer satisfaction is, of course, a critical issue for most companies. In part, this is because client satisfaction is often a key driver that affects repeat sales. Also, bad experiences suggest that the customer will not recommend the product or company to their friends.

For instance, many customers complete their evaluation regarding a hotel's service level after they have checked out. They might use a paper version and mail the form in. However, increasingly clients use some type of online platform, such as TripAdvisor, to share their evaluation with the public. Accordingly, the hotel might not even hear the good news, because it might not be posted on its own Web site, but

Table 7.4 Customer satisfaction—input and output

#	Rating	Questions about contentment: What customers need and want matters	Points
7.4.1	*****	Does the organization collect feedback from customers about output (e.g., how is it perceived)?	0, 1, 2, or 3
7.4.2	*****	Does the firm collect customer feedback about how well the output clients receive meets their requirements (e.g., is the pdf file's content relevant, of value)?	...
7.4.3	*****	Does the organization assess how well certain social media marketing processes work (e.g., answering incoming requests for help via e-mail, Twitter, or blog post works well because...)?	...
7.4.4	*****	Does the organization conduct random exit surveys that ask website/blog visitors to answer a few short questions?	...
7.4.5	*****	Does the exit survey ask visitors if they found the information they came looking for?	...
7.4.6	*****	Does data collected from customers provide information about how satisfied they were with the process (e.g., was it easy to fill in the form, useful, did I get help sending an e-mail or tweeting)?	...

Note: Please remember that the above set of questions can be used for each single social media marketing activities, such as answering customer inquiries, suggestions, cries for help with a special Facebook page, as well as each separate Twitter account or blog. Put differently, you may choose to use the above list to get an overall assessment or a detailed one for each different part of your social media marketing activities

The total number of points can range from 0 to 3 for each item, which is then multiplied by the number of stars given, ranging from 1 to 5. The range of scores for each item is therefore 0 to 15, which is then multiplied by the number of questions. Accordingly, for the above table, the maximum score is 6 (questions) × 15 = 90

For more information about the calculations, scaling, and rationale, please see Table 5.1

elsewhere. Of course, monitoring these sentiments (positive or negative) will ensure that we get this information.

Table 7.4 provides a template that allows a systematic assessment of these challenges, but it also requires that we ask clients to provide feedback regarding the process and the output. For instance, how useful are the FAQs, checklists on the Web site, support via the Web-based form, etc. to our clients? In the case of the tweet from Migros telling me to phone the hotline, the result was me not signing up at all (Gattiker, Urs E. February 12, 2012), another customer who experienced the company as unhelpful.

7.5 Mistakes and Nonconformities

A *nonconformity is a failure to comply with a requirement* of a company's quality system regarding a particular process. Of course, this might also apply to regulatory requirements as stipulated by the Securities and Exchange Commission (SEC), an

Table 7.5 Mistakes and nonconformities

#	Rating	Questions	Score
7.5.1	*****	Do you collect information about output nonconformities (e.g., below standard, mistakes, violates guidelines)?	0, 1, 2, or 3
7.5.2	*****	Do you collect information how well outputs meet requirements (e.g., quality levels or speed of reply regarding customer inquiry)?	…
7.5.3	*****	Do you have a method in place that helps minimize at reasonable cost the risk for nonconforming output (i.e., making the risk manageable)?	…
7.5.4	*****	Does the team have the resources needed to implement and manage this process (i.e., minimizing risks and keeping on top of nonconformity incidents)?	…
7.5.5	*****	Does the organization have a procedure in place that assures that these incidents are being used for further skills upgrading or training sessions with staff?	…

Note: Please remember, that the above set of questions can be used for each single social media marketing activity, such as answering customer inquiries, suggestions, cries for help on a special Facebook page, exactly as well as each separate Twitter account or blog. Put differently, you may choose to use the above list to get an overall assessment or a detailed one for each different part of your social media marketing activities

The total number of points can range from 0 to 3 for each item, which is then multiplied by the number of stars given, ranging from 1 to 5. The range of scores for each item is therefore 0 to 15, which is then multiplied by the number of questions. Accordingly, for the above table, the maximum score is 5 (questions) × 15 = 75

For more information about the calculations, scaling, and rationale, please see Table 5.1

important regulatory agency in the US for financial matters. For instance, it stipulates what kind of social media activity must be archived by the finance industry and how to do so and be compliant (see more at bottom of http://info.cytrap.eu/terms-privacy/sm-policy).

Being online does entail some risks of making mistakes or producing output that does not conform to the company's standard. For instance, it may be that an employee uses software that allows them to send out a tweet to their personal account or the company's. But the style of their private tweets may be quite different than what the employee uses when tweeting on the corporate Twitter account.

To illustrate, on a Friday evening an American Red Cross worker sent a tweet suggesting that he would have a few beers with friends. Unfortunately, he pushed the wrong button and by mistake the tweet went out on the organization's Twitter account. How should the organization respond to such a nonconformity? This is what needs to be evaluated to develop a procedure on how to deal with this properly. Naturally, nonconformity cases should be used to facilitate the team's education, to reduce such occurrences. Of course, this also helps staff be ready for this eventuality should it happen again. In turn, the team can manage this risk and possible disaster effectively (see Table 7.8) (Gattiker, Urs E. April 4, 2011).

As Table 7.5 would suggest, nonconformities and mistakes such as those described above must be archived. Moreover, we should document discussions with staff about such cases and whether training was provided to reduce the chances of reoccurrence.

7.6 Compliance and Record Keeping

Compliance is about running a business and delivering products in ways that are fair and ethical. Compliance is a state in which a *process or activity is conducted in accordance with established guidelines, specifications, or legislation.* Areas that are particularly important here include data protection and privacy regulation, and e-commerce regulation as they pertain to your industry. Often, national regulation is no longer sufficient to protect the company from risks that could become costly mistakes involving unnecessary litigation.

For European companies, it is probably of interest to address this issue using local regulation as well as EU regulation. Moreover, in some businesses, EU member states or other jurisdictions (e.g., State of California) may be trail blazers (e.g., German data protection legislation, Province of Ontario, Canada—privacy protection). Keeping an eye on these players is a useful way to ensure that your process follows regulation from these places that tend to set trends (e.g., California or Ontario).

Compliance requires that we make sure we can produce a paper trail with the documents which *indicate to others that we have done what we are supposed to do. E-discovery might necessitate that we produce chat logs or tweets* sent on our account. While these things are costly for SMEs, it is probably better to carefully assess the risks the company takes by not archiving such information. During e-discovery, the organization might simply not be able to produce the documentation the court wants which could have some costly and embarrassing consequences, and damage the organization's reputation.

Table 7.6 provides a set of questions that need to be discussed and evaluated to ensure that compliance and record keeping are up to standards.

Table 7.6 Compliance and record keeping

#	Rating	Questions	Points
7.6.1	*****	Do you keep a record of how nonconforming process outputs are identified (e.g., are these logged or registered)?	0, 1, 2, or 3
7.6.2	*****	Do you keep a record of how nonconforming process outputs are controlled (e.g., in order for the company to manage these risks)?	...
7.6.3	*****	Can you demonstrate that this process of compliance management produces the output intended?	...
7.6.4	*****	Can you demonstrate that this process management portion focusing on compliance produces the compliant output?	...
7.6.5	*****	Are process inputs such as using a URL linking to a pdf or Web site verified to see if they meet requirements before starting the process (e.g., retweeting the link, putting link on the Web site or blog)?	...

(continued)

Table 7.6 (continued)

#	Rating	Questions	Points
7.6.6	*****	Are process inputs discussed between those members producing it and those possibly sharing with clients (e.g., writing a Web page entry about it, putting it into the news)?	...
7.6.7	*****	Do internal parties review content (e.g., does it meet regulatory requirements, data protection regulation) that will be shared with clients and others before the social sharing is done?	...

Note: Please remember, that the above set of questions can be used for each single social media marketing activity, such as answering customer inquiries, suggestions, cries for help on a special Facebook page, exactly as well as each separate Twitter account or blog. Put differently, you may choose to use the above list to get an overall assessment or a detailed one for each different part of your social media marketing activities

The total number of points can range from 0 to 3 for each item, which is then multiplied by the number of stars given, ranging from 1 to 5. The range of scores for each item is therefore 0 to 15, which is then multiplied by the number of questions. Accordingly, for the above table, the maximum score is 7 (questions) × 15 = 105

For more information about the calculations, scaling, and rationale, please see Table 5.1

7.7 Successful Compliance

In order to foster compliance, we need to make sure that our staff have the skill set required to be compliant. In other words, how do they know what is correct and what violates standards?

When one is faced with an ethical problem or a difficult situation on the social Web, our *Social Media Guidelines* (see http://info.cytrap.eu/?page_id=686) suggest that you ask yourself these four questions before going ahead with sharing:

– Would I consider it personally *embarrassing or unpleasant* if my colleagues heard about this (e.g., tweet, blog comment)?
– Could I be considered to have *unfairly benefitted* from this activity due *solely to my organizational position*?
– Could my *company's reputation suffer* if the media or competitors get hold of this?
– Could the *client, friend, or foe be upset* by receiving my tweet, e-mail, or comment on Google+ for instance because they feel *talked down to or brushed off*?

It is clear that staff must receive the training needed to understand the above and know how it works in practice. Table 7.7 lists the questions that must be answered during an audit.

Table 7.7 also provides a set of questions that permit the systematic evaluation of how we try to foster success for our staff and their social media efforts, while making sure that we are compliant with pertinent regulation. Unless you provide your team with some training they have to learn by doing and the generally entails learning from mistakes. However, discussing the latter during training sessions (e.g., brown bag lunch or lunch buffet provided by company—let us discuss) is probably a safer way to get a handle on this challenge than using a wait and see attitude.

Table 7.7 Fostering compliance and building the necessary skill set

#	Rating	Questions	Points
7.7.1	*****	Do you empower new staff to acquire the skills needed to use social media according to guidelines?	0, 1, 2, or 3
7.7.2	*****	Did your employees get the chance to upgrade their skills about communicating with clients using social media (e.g., when to tweet, what kind of tweets and how often)?	...
7.7.3	*****	Do your staff understand that a blog comment left by a reader must be replied to using appropriate language (e.g., doing it within 12 hours, 7 days a week)?	...
7.7.4	*****	Were staff trained on what to do when a crisis unfolds on some social media channel (e.g., Facebook—group attacking your brand, distributing wrong information, rumor mill is going rampant)?	...
7.7.5	*****	Are staff trained about what inappropriate behavior (e.g., language) consists of, with the help of examples and cases?	...

Note: Please remember, that the above set of questions can be used for each single social media marketing activity, such as answering customer inquiries, suggestions, cries for help on a special Facebook page, exactly as well as each separate Twitter account or blog. Put differently, you may choose to use the above list to get an overall assessment or a detailed one for each different part of your social media marketing activities

The total number of points can range from 0 to 3 for each item, which is then multiplied by the number of stars given, ranging from 1 to 5. The range of scores for each item is therefore 0 to 15, which is then multiplied by the number of questions. Accordingly, for the above table, the maximum score is 5 (questions) × 15 = 75

For more information about the calculations, scaling, and rationale, please see Table 5.1

7.8 Crisis Management Resources

Social media has become a sphere were misinformation, gossip, rumors, or bad-mouthing can spread very quickly. Accordingly, the organization needs to be able to respond in a timely fashion to such developments. This means that the organization is able to answer a question from those that want to hear the facts and truth within a reasonable amount of time. Of course, misinformation is totally unacceptable as is waiting until Monday when staff are back at the office.

When the crisis happens, providing information that illustrates why things are different than presented by some can do wonders. Unfortunately, unless such a response is quick in coming, the avalanche of rumors and urban legends is likely to totally drown out the company's reply. An example of how quick that can happen was the Greenpeace attack against Nestlé's KitKat brand (read more here: http://commetrics.com/?p=7607).

Table 7.8 outlines what steps must be taken by the organization to be ready for any type of disaster such as the company being attacked in social media for something it did or did not do. The questions address some of the pertinent issues, including but not limited to having a checklist and knowing whom to call and where to get the information needed to counter the attack with facts that may help clarify the issue. Similarly, if clients complain, a procedure needs to be in place detailing what steps can be taken to help them and rectify their problem.

Table 7.8 Crisis management: Testing your capabilities for effective response

#	Rating	Questions	Points
7.8.1	*****	Is there a checklist on how to handle negative sentiment (e.g., about your staff, product, brand) in the social media sphere *that allows staff to pull the emergency handle* for taking action?	0, 1, 2, or 3
7.8.2	*****	Is there a plan for how to handle negative sentiment (e.g., about your staff, product, brand) in the social media sphere with an *orchestrated and quick response* (by whom)?	...
7.8.3	*****	By monitoring sentiment on various channels (see also Table 6.8) regarding comments about firm, brand, product, and staff, do you have a *tried and tested procedure* in place *permitting a response with an appropriate time lag* (even during public holidays, weekends, etc., within 12 hours)?	...
7.8.4	*****	By monitoring sentiment on various channels (see also Table 6.8) regarding comments about firm, brand, product, and staff, do you have a *tried and tested procedure* in place permitting a response that *provides the complaining party with factual information to help them solve the problem* (e.g., link to FAQ, phone number, getting an in-house expert to call them)?	...

Note: Please remember, that the above set of questions can be used for each single social media marketing activity, such as answering customer inquiries, suggestions, cries for help on a special Facebook page, exactly as well as each separate Twitter account or blog. Put differently, you may choose to use the above list to get an overall assessment or a detailed one for each different part of your social media marketing activities

The total number of points can range from 0 to 3 for each item, which is then multiplied by the number of stars given, ranging from 1 to 5. The range of scores for each item is therefore 0 to 15, which is then multiplied by the number of questions. Accordingly, for the above table, the maximum score is 4 (questions) × 15 = 60

For more information about the calculations, scaling and rationale, please see Table 5.1

7.9   Monitoring and Measuring

We pointed out in Chapter 5 that a *major risk the company has to deal with is that an overreliance on technology is a recipe for failure.* Using software like Hotsuite or My.ComMetrics.com is helpful to assess how well you are performing but, unless this is guided by a strategy and operational goals with measures that use actionable metrics, the results might not be that useful. Unless collecting data about pageviews results in action if you do not achieve the objective, why worry about it? Put differently, why should your boss care about 100,000 pageviews (see http://commetrics. com/?p=13427)? The challenge is to be able to measure how your 100,000 Facebook friends or Twitter followers can actually improve customer retention and reduce product recalls.

The above challenge is also illustrated with a tool like Twitter, which has an abundance of measuring tools, but only a small group provides you with insight needed to help you improve. Navel-gazing metrics might make you feel great but do little if anything for your bottom line (Gattiker, Urs E. April 1, 2012).

Table 7.9 Monitoring and measuring

#	Rating	Questions	Points
7.9.1	*****	Do you maintain a record of your monitoring activities, such as the validity of process monitoring efforts (do these metrics measure what they are supposed to)?	0, 1, 2, or 3
7.9.2	*****	Do you maintain a record of your monitoring activities, such as the reliability/replicability of process monitoring efforts (e.g., are you able to repeat this finding taking another measure–repeatability)?	…
7.9.3	*****	Do you maintain a record of your monitoring activities, such as what is being measured at repeatable intervals (e.g., monthly statistics about visitors or downloads of a white paper)?	…
7.9.4	*****	Do you take corrective actions if measurement activities do not meet objectives as planned?	…
7.9.5	*****	Do you evaluate your monitoring and measurement activities regularly to see where improvement is needed?	…

Note: Please remember, that the above set of questions can be used for each single social media marketing activity, such as answering customer inquiries, suggestions, cries for help on a special Facebook page, exactly as well as each separate Twitter account or blog. Put differently, you may choose to use the above list to get an overall assessment or a detailed one for each different part of your social media marketing activities

The total number of points can range from 0 to 3 for each item, which is then multiplied by the number of stars given, ranging from 1 to 5. The range of scores for each item is therefore 0 to 15, which is then multiplied by the number of questions. Accordingly, for the above table, the maximum score is 5 (questions) × 15 = 75

For more information about the calculations, scaling, and rationale, please see Table 5.1

Table 7.9 outlines how the process regarding the activities in social media marketing should be evaluated. Both validity (measuring the right stuff) as well as reliability (can it be replicated—are the results the same if repeated a week later?) of measuring and monitoring efforts must be checked. Table 7.9 lists some of these questions. While you can add more than the five broad questions listed, avoid making things too detailed and cumbersome. The list is to be understood as a guideline to get you to ask the right questions to uncover strengths and weaknesses.

7.10   Conclusion

With the templates and questions provided in this chapter, you should be in the position to conduct a social media audit. It should be easy to adjust the templates to fit your company's context, industry, and regulatory environment.

Of increasing importance is being compliant with national and international regulation. These issues are addressed and using the questions provided will allow you to focus on them, especially if nonconformities are used as valuable case studies. These will help you and your team improve performance and reduce the risk for possible nonconformities and public relations disasters that damage the organization's reputation.

Chapter 8 will address how you can systematically take information collected in Chapter 7 to continuously improve the use of social media activities and marketing processes in your organization.

References

Gattiker, Urs E. (Not dated). Governance. [Blog page – info.CyTRAP.eu]. Retrieved January 19, 2012, from http://info.cytrap.eu//?page_id=59

Gattiker, Urs E. (February 12, 2012). Social CRM: Kundenservice mit Twitter (Social CRM: Customer service with Twitter) [Blog post—info.CyTRAP.eu] Retrieved February 25, 2012, from http://info.cytrap.eu/?p=3122/

Gattiker, Urs E. (March 14, 2011). Measuring Facebook engagement. [Blog post—ComMetrics]. Retrieved January 15, 2012, from http://commetrics.com/?p=14257

Gattiker, Urs E. (April 4, 2011). Can cause marketing damage reputations [Blog post—ComMetrics]. Retrieved April 4, 2012, from http://commetrics.com/?p=14738

Gattiker, Urs E. (October 6, 2011). My bank loves me NOT [Blog post—ComMetrics]. Retrieved January 15, 2012, from http://commetrics.com/?p=16836

Gattiker, Urs E. (April 1, 2012). Twitter metrics: The ultimate tools (Social CRM: Customer service with Twitter) [Blog post—info.CyTRAP.eu] Retrieved April 3, 2012, from http://commetrics.com/?p=2089

Chapter 8
Continuous Improvement

Abstract Improvement of the processes we use for social media marketing and social sharing is critical to leverage our resources. Nevertheless, relevancy plays a key role, requiring that we address the critical issues first. Moreover, relevancy means that the metrics, key performance indicators (KPIs), or key drivers used have to relate to things that matter (e.g., customer satisfaction, number of days between repeat sales orders, referrals). For most SMEs, it cannot be about eyeballs unless they are potential clients and ultimately create revenue for the company.

Measuring things is an important activity that most organizations require. It helps ensure that the train is still on track to reach its target, but we still have to verify our route is the right one as we travel it. Accordingly, in Chapter 7, we focused on the quality assurance process. The focus was on finding out if our objectives were achieved, but most importantly, whether the process for doing so met our quality standards.

Of course, the breadth, depth, and scope of our audit matters and so does context (small versus large enterprise). Once we have addressed this, we must plan how we can make use of data collected, such as with the templates in Chapters 4 to 7, to improve the process further. We want to see if these data could be used to improve our train's speed and/or reduce our energy consumption further. If this were to be accomplished, we would arrive at our destination earlier and/or save fuel that we can use otherwise. For the social media context, this means sifting through these data to find insights that allow us to better allocate resources. As a result, the effectiveness of our activities increases, and allows us to use resources smarter.

An important suggestion here is also to *take minutes of the discussions held for each of the questions included.* These structured notes, that *should be no more than a half typed page for each question,* can help clarify the decision making process for others. As importantly, it *helps to make sure that the team agrees, and understands and supports the decision.*

This approach has been shown to significantly improve decisions in contexts like school admissions and hiring (Milkman et al. 2009). Of course, this will *allow the team to consider multiple options simultaneously rather than separately.* Again, this follows best practice grounded in research. The latter also demonstrates that this can optimize outcomes and increase the team's willpower for carrying out a choice made for social media activities.

8.1   Reviewing the Data

Once the audit is completed, including a thorough assessment of quality (see Chapter 7), we need to sift through the data we have collected. We need to try to make sense out of it before making decisions. The questions in Table 8.1 list the issues that we must address toward the end of the audit cycle when using the *CySoMAT*.

To illustrate this matter further, our *audit may have revealed nonconformities* regarding inputs and outputs. Before we embark on preventive action to reduce this risk, however, it is recommended we also seek feedback about what we intend to change, particularly from those depending upon the input and output. We need to talk to suppliers and/or clients as well as other departments.

For instance, if a person sends an e-mail to the company's overall e-mail address, such as info [at] company [dot] com, who sifts through these e-mails? How will this person analyze these mails and decide what to do? For instance, will the e-mails go to the hotel reception? Will reception staff answer all e-mails or not? Whatever works, we have to decide and we cannot be certain that each employee will be as motivated, sensible, and smart as the next one or those who have worked with us for several years.

Even when the mail gets forwarded, how do we make sure that the recipient actually answers it? Will the person from reception that decided to forward the e-mail in-house get a cc when the reply goes out? As well, what kind of response does the sender receive? Will there be a follow-up call or e-mail or both? Within what time frame will we reply? If Twitter or Facebook requests are answered within a couple of hours, how about e-mails? As we have noted elsewhere, we cannot deal with certain channels differently, such as answering faster because the person asked in public using Twitter instead of via e-mail. In both cases, Twitter or e-mail, the client expects a speedy reply and wants the answer quickly. Of course, if I need some help with a bill about an item charge I do not understand, an e-mail within 48 hours will do as long as the answer is helpful and explains. If I want to connect my cable modem to watch TV, 48 hours waiting for support and help will not do.

By looking at how we handle the incoming e-mail, process it, and draft a reply (output), we may find things we want to change. It could be that the quality of the process needs improvement, such as the quality of the reply provided. In this case, the replies might have to be changed, such as improving format, information included, and the structure of the reply. A good way to improve is to first get feedback from those affected. This helps draft changes that will further support our efforts in reducing nonconformities or replies that may not meet the standards we set for ourselves (e.g., timeliness and quality of reply). Addressing the issues outlined in Table 8.1 helps further improve the process.

Table 8.1 Sifting through data that were collected

#	Rating	Continuously improving the process subsequent to the audit	Points
8.1.1	*****	Audit information is being systematically used	0, 1, 2, or 3
8.1.2	*****	There is a management review of audit findings	...
8.1.3	*****	Audit findings are being discussed with process owner or team	...
8.1.4	*****	Audit findings are being shared with process clients (e.g., readers and users) in order to collect their feedback	...
8.1.5	*****	Input from process customers regarding preventive action (e.g., nonconformities of output generated as evaluated during audit) is collected as part of the review of audit findings	...
8.1.6	*****	Input from process suppliers for preventive action regarding nonconformities of input as reported in audit is collected as part of the review of audit findings	...
8.1.7	*****	Feedback regarding possible changes to be introduced in the process to reduce the number of nonconformities is planned and part of the review of audit findings	...

Note: Please remember that the above set of questions can be used for each single social media marketing activity, such as answering customer inquiries, suggestions, and cries for help on a special Facebook page, exactly as well as each separate Twitter account or blog. Put differently, you may choose to use the above list to get an overall assessment or a detailed one for each different part of your social media marketing activities

The total number of points can range from 0 to 3 for each item, which is then multiplied by the number of stars given, ranging from 1 to 5. The range of scores for each item is therefore 0 to 15, which is then multiplied by the number of questions. Accordingly, for the above table, the maximum score is 7 (questions) × 15 = 105

For more information about the calculations, scaling, and rationale, please see Table 5.1

8.2 Applying Methods and Measurement

Based on the information and discussions held as systemized in Table 8.1, we can then assess how the process could be changed. We also need to make sure that we measure from the audit/baseline to see if things improve or not.

In this context, a *small change* of the process might be adding another person to the team managing the Twitter account (i.e., those allowed to tweet from the company's Twitter account). *A more substantial change* could be if you decide to reduce the number of tweets from about four each day to one. You could try to schedule your tweets during times of the day clients may prefer receiving them, such as 7:00 or 8:00 AM and 11:00 AM on workdays. On Sunday, you might shift to about 9:30 AM to catch people while having their breakfast. Thank you tweets about mentions and retweets (RTs) are scheduled to go out on Saturdays, when most people are not on Twitter. While this avoids clogging their feed, those being thanked will get a notice by Twitter or another service about being mentioned anyway so, they will be pleased.

The questions raised in Table 8.2 need to be discussed to enable the team to decide what changes may be warranted. Here, the *focus should be on those changes*

Table 8.2 Making inferences to move forward

#	Rating	Questions—taking the findings from the audit and review to improve performance (see Chapters 4–7)	Points
8.2.1	*****	Are the changes being monitored in order to plot subsequent improvements (e.g., number of visitors, positive sentiment, pageviews, and conversion)?	0, 1, 2, or 3
8.2.2	*****	Are the audit results used as the baseline for moving forward and to improve (e.g., chart out the trend and see if it moves in the right direction)?	...
8.2.3	*****	Are methods applied for corrective actions that help improve performance regarding KPIs?	...
8.2.4	*****	Is an impact analysis done regarding the changes that were implemented to improve performance?	...
8.2.5	*****	Are you planning to make a *small* change to this process? If so, what small changes are planned and what impact are you hoping to accomplish with them?	...
8.2.6	*****	Are you planning to change the process? What changes are planned and what impact are you hoping to accomplish with them?	...
8.2.7	*****	When changing this process, are you checking that the integrity of the process can and is being maintained?	...
8.2.8	*****	Do you assure documentation of possible improvements of key metrics used to measure the changed process (e.g., reduced waiting times and fewer calls to customer support)?	...

Note: Please remember that the above set of questions can be used for each single social media marketing activity, such as answering customer inquiries, suggestions, and cries for help on a special Facebook page, exactly as well as each separate Twitter account or blog. Put differently, you may choose to use the above list to get an overall assessment or a detailed one for each different part of your social media marketing activities

The total number of points can range from 0 to 3 for each item, which is then multiplied by the number of stars given, ranging from 1 to 5. The range of scores for each item is therefore 0 to 15, which is then multiplied by the number of questions. Accordingly, for the above table, the maximum score is 8 (questions) × 15 = 120

For more information about the calculations, scaling, and rationale, please see Table 5.1

that are required to stay compliant. Nevertheless, there might be others where the *effort is relatively small, but the effect could be substantial.* An example is shifting tweeting times to reach more of your followers as measured with the clicks on the shortened URLs you sent.

8.3   Reviewing Strategy and Key Performance Indicators

How do we go about it if we know that less than half a percent of Facebook fans who identify themselves as Liking a brand actually bother to create any content for it? An example of creating content would be if they comment on wall posts or re-share by writing a short note before posting on their own wall for their friends to see (see Gattiker, Urs E. February 5, 2012).

Table 8.3 Reviewing strategy and KPIs—linking to key operators

#	Rating	Continuously improving the process subsequent to the audit	Points
8.3.1	*****	Do you review strategy and KPIs to make sure their link to key operators (e.g., customer satisfaction, product returns) justifies spending resources on improving performance?	0, 1, 2, or 3
8.3.2	*****	Are the three top inputs from social media (e.g., Facebook page, Web site, and blog) still driving performance targets we care about (e.g., customer retention, returns, micro-conversions, and marketing leads)?	…
8.3.3	*****	Have we assessed whether our 3–5 operating metrics used for social media marketing are closely linked to (or correlate with) the most important drivers of value creation for our organization (e.g., leads or request for product information sent via online form)?	…
8.3.4	*****	Do the resources we spend for social media marketing to maintain a Facebook, Google+, Tumblr, or Second Life page or destination allow us to reach 20% or more of our customers?	…
8.3.5	*****	Do our top three destinations on the social Web (e.g., Facebook page, corporate blog, and/or Flickr) result in engagement or levels of resonance that are better than average (e.g., around 0.5% on Facebook)?	…
8.3.6	*****	Do our social media efforts and contributions help make the customer experience more convenient (e.g., before and during sale, as well as afterwards, such as getting help or warranty work done)?	…

Note: Please remember that the clearer the guidance provided by this strategic review of KPIs and their link to key operators, the more effectively scarce resources can be spent to improve only those things regarding social media that help improve the bottom line. Some difficult choices will have to be made

The total number of points can range from 0 to 3 for each item, which is then multiplied by the number of stars given, ranging from 1 to 5. The range of scores for each item is therefore 0 to 15, which is then multiplied by the number of questions. Accordingly, for the above table, the maximum score is 6 (questions) × 15 = 90

For more information about the calculations, scaling, and rationale, please see Table 5.1

In most cases, we cannot be active on many platforms due to budget constraints, and while Second Life was once the darling of the industry, this is no longer the case - platforms come and go for various reasons. For instance, Google purchased Aardvark just to close it down about 18 months after it had paid over 50 million US dollars (see more here: http://www.flickr.com/photos/measure-for-impact/6237231742/). Accordingly, there is no guarantee that our contributions on the Quora platform (ask questions to get answers from pros) will not experience the same fate in a year.

Table 8.3 also points out that we need to address whether the tools or platforms we use enjoy a level of diffusion that allows us to reach 20% or 30% of our clients.

It also requires that we assess if *the metrics used are still linked to the overall strategies* (e.g., how does measuring × help improve sales by 10% next year?). Based on the audit results, we need to review if what we have done over the last quarter or 6 months still gets us where we wish to go.

The above illustrates that we have to address if our activities on various platforms are *like broadcasting to an empty football stadium* (i.e., nobody is listening) or *if people pay attention and engage with us* (e.g., commenting). We need to look at the metrics and possibly decide to realign our resources or refocus our social media activities. The questions in Table 8.3 help you do this in a systematic way. It is Critical that we also focus on whether social media activities are still correlated or linked to those key drivers top management really cares about (e.g., customer satisfaction, customer returns, or average size of order). Unless this is accomplished, why should we improve something that does not affect our bottom line?

8.4 Managing the Improvement Process

We all know several instances where a possible public relations disaster turned into a real crisis. Improvements require that we:

1. Analyze the problems identified by the audit process.
2. Prioritize the tasks to be undertaken.

In other words, the company may rearrange the process problems as identified by the social media audit. Before this can be done, however, we need to prioritize the things that need attention. Due to time constraints as well as budgetary limitations, it might be that not everything can be done quickly. Using our prioritized list, the *company has to decide what warrants attention first due to risk concerns or compliance matters*. Furthermore, some things *may be improved by small changes that require neither much investment nor time to improve performance*.

Accordingly, a careful balance of these priorities is necessary to *accomplish the most with the least amount of resources* while *assuring good governance and being compliant*.

Table 8.4 outlines some of the questions that need to be addressed in a systematic fashion to get a handle on issues that were identified. The managing of this process also requires that training needs, as identified, are addressed with the appropriate skills-upgrading opportunities for staff. Issues regarding nonconformities, governance, and compliance are high on the priority list and will have to be addressed.

Table 8.4 Managing the improvement process

#	Rating	Are we handling this process systematically and making changes following our list of prioritized actions?	Points
8.4.1	*****	Does your process owner or manager ensure that what we prioritize the identified process problems and stick with that list?	0, 1, 2, or 3
8.4.2	*****	Does the process owner ensure that problems identified by auditors are being analyzed and prioritized with the timeline to get resolution?	...
8.4.3	*****	Are customers, clients, and employees made aware of the changes that will occur with a communication plan?	...
8.4.4	*****	Is how the training plan to improve the process will affect each employee assessed to assure that they improve their skills as needed?	...
8.4.5	*****	Are we making sure that eliminating the process problems will reduce the risks for nonconformities?	...
8.4.6	*****	Do the changes reduce the occurrence of undesirable consequences of the process?	...
8.4.7	*****	Do the changes reduce the occurrence of outcomes that may cause compliance issues (e.g., privacy, intellectual property, other pertinent laws and regulations)?	...
8.4.8	*****	Are these remedial actions taken in a timely manner?	...
8.4.9	*****	Did we put together a budget to rectify the prioritized process problems?	...

Note: Please remember that the clearer the guidance provided by this strategic review of KPIs and their link to key operators, the more effectively scarce resources can be spent to improve only those things regarding social media that help improve the bottom line. Some difficult choices will have to be made

The total number of points can range from 0 to 3 for each, which is then multiplied by the number of stars given, ranging from 1 to 5. The range of scores for each item is therefore 0 to 15, which is then multiplied by the number of questions. Accordingly, for the above table, the maximum score is 9 (questions) × 15 = 135

For more information about the calculations, scaling, and rationale, please see Table 5.1

8.5 Implementing Suggestions for Change

If you decide to improve performance, you have to manage the process carefully and systematically. Not only do you have to *set a timeline and a budget* to get the changes implemented, you also have to *address the matter regarding governance, compliance, and nonconformities*. If the audit shows that to manage Twitter better you need to add several more people to the account on a rotating schedule for weekends, what are the *chances that this increases the risks for making mistakes* (e.g., tweeting a private message on the corporate account by accident)? Could this complicate matters, and if so, how can the chances for possible nonconformities be reduced? As well, does the budget allow for this?

If we implement changes, such as adding a special Facebook page that just handles customer inquiries, we need to address how the process of replying can be

Table 8.5 Implementing suggestions for change

#	Rating	Managing the actual implementation process of changes identified by the audit in a systematic and speedy way	Points
8.5.1	*****	Does the team systematically implement and keep track of progress made toward implementing prioritized suggestions for changes?	0, 1, 2, or 3
8.5.2	*****	Are we improving the management of this change process?	…
8.5.3	*****	Are we improving the control of the implementation of the prioritized suggestions for changes?	…
8.5.4	*****	Do we need to improve our process infrastructure?	…
8.5.5	*****	Do forthcoming changes require additional tools and software (or improvements)?	…
8.5.6	*****	Do current support levels need adjustment to account for the coming changes?	…
8.5.7	*****	Will actions that are lower on the priority list but still considered important be completed within a given and agreed upon timeframe?	…
8.5.8	*****	Did we put together an itemized budget to spell out the resources needed to rectify the prioritized process problems?	…

Note: Please remember, the clearer the guidance from the management review, the more helpful it will be to the efforts taken for improvement of the process. For instance, what is adequacy or effectiveness in this context, or how we define and measure this, needs to be specified. What is acceptable performance or not must be understood

The total number of points can range from 0 to 3 for each item, which is then multiplied by the number of stars given, ranging from 1 to 5. The range of scores for each item is therefore 0 to 15, which is then multiplied by the number of questions. Accordingly, for the above table, the maximum score is 8 (questions) × 15 = 120

For more information about the calculations, scaling, and rationale, please see Table 5.1

handled. If local Facebook pages are needed to allow the use of several languages, then to manage the process swiftly, each country needs to have several people that monitor comments and reply accordingly.

Table 8.5 outlines the questions we need to ask ourselves before embarking on implementing the suggestions derived from the audit data. Sifting through and analyzing data may suggest certain things. However, to *do it systematically and within budget*, things in Table 8.5 need to be addressed by the team. Besides the time angle that needs addressing, a budget needs to be put in place to rectify possible software or infrastructure issues to mention two possibilities.

8.6 Improving Crisis Management

As we pointed out earlier, crisis management is an important issue that warrants some thorough work. Chapter 7, specifically Table 7.8, addressed whether we had the capabilities in place to respond adequately to a crisis building on social media,

Table 8.6 Improving crisis management

#	Rating	Continuously improving the process subsequent to the audit to be better prepared to handle a crisis that could severely damage our *reputation*	Score
8.6.1	*****	Where the crisis management capabilities tested with a fire drill?	0, 1, 2, or 3
8.6.2	*****	Do we have a process in place for learning from experience(s) by systematically recording what we do and how to *resolve process problems*?	…
8.6.3	*****	Are we learning from experience by systematically recording what we do and how to resolve identified *problems* (e.g., what went wrong last time)?	…
8.6.4	*****	Are we using client feedback to systematically analyze the changes that are required (e.g., is our communication clear enough to minimize the risk for misunderstandings by clients)?	…
8.6.5	*****	Did we put together an itemized budget to spell out the resources needed to rectify the prioritized process problems that hinder our more effective crisis management?	…

Note: Please remember, the clearer the guidance from the management review, the more helpful it will be to the efforts taken for improvement of the process. For instance, what is adequacy or effectiveness in this context, or how we define and measure this, needs to be specified. What is acceptable performance or not must be understood

The total number of points can range from 0 to 3 for each item, which is then multiplied by the number of stars given, ranging from 1 to 5. The range of scores for each item is therefore 0 to 15, which is then multiplied by the number of questions. Accordingly, for the above table, the maximum score is 5 (questions) × 15 = 75

For more information about the calculations, scaling, and rationale, please see Table 5.1

such as our Facebook page being filled up with comments by angry customers. Table 8.6 tries to put this in practice and go a step further.

To illustrate, outdoor equipment and clothing manufacturer Mammut, has worked hard on its image as a green company. Unfortunately, the company joined a loby group that wanted to steer clear of a proposed CO_2 tax that went to referendum in Switzerland. While the company might be correct that such a tax on CO_2 emissions is not an effective way to cut emissions unless it is done around the globe, customers were not amused. It raised a storm of negative comments on Facebook. The company was slow in responding and while it should be congratulated for doing so, its bulletin came across as inauthentic and being written by lawyers (Gattiker, Urs E. September 7, 2011, see section *Live your corporate image and manage a reputation crisis smartly*).

Table 8.6 should help you assess if the procedures and processes in place have a chance of *surviving a real-life onslaught* that could cause serious damage to your reputation. Without testing these procedures and getting feedback from friends and foes about how you are doing, improvement is difficult.

Just as when you conduct a fire drill, sometimes you find out that things are not up to standards. This is what Netflix did when it pretty much reversed its earlier decision about how it would continue delivering TV and music content over the internet (see http://www.flickr.com/photos/measure-for-impact/6171418085). It tried to manage the disaster, but also put procedures in place to be better prepared if this or something similar were ever to happen again.

What we think is vital is that the crisis management capabilities are tested with something similar to a fire drill to ensure it works. For instance, what is supposed to happen if a worker inadvertently publishes a private tweet on the corporate account? To illustrate, a Chrysler employee published "I find it ironic that Detroit is known as the #motorcity and yet no one here knows how to fucking drive" on the ChryslerAuto Twitter account. Should the company then delete the tweet, issue a public apology on its blog and, in addition, fire the employee (Rick 2011)? What if the above tweet was sent out in error? Should the employee really be fired or could this possibly cause a backlash in public opinion? Things like this will happen, so the company must have a system in place that makes it possible to address such disasters quickly, fairly, and systematically.

8.7   Further Improving Reputation

Jeff Bezos, the founder of Amazon, is attributed to having made this statement: *"Your reputation is what people say about you when you are not in the room."*

Richard Branson, founder of the Virgin Group, is credited with this statement: *"Build brands not around products, but around reputation,"* (see Gattiker, Urs E. August 6, 2008)

Put simply, brand is what the corporation tells us about itself or the product and what it wants and aspires to be. Reputation is what people feel about the company. They are two sides of the same coin.

More formally, reputation is the collective representation of multiple constituencies' perception of the corporation's behavior. Accordingly, reputation is about how efforts regarding brand and what the company has done or delivered are seen by its various constituencies (e.g., investors, costumers, employees, and consumer advocates).

Table 8.7 provides a small set of questions that will guide you through this challenge in a systematic way. In particular, we need to analyze what efforts are undertaken to improve how our staff represent themselves and the company on various platforms. For instance, do they actively contribute to the Xing or LinkedIn groups they are members of? Groups do not need free-riders (i.e., those that might read the content, but rarely if ever contribute to the live discussion and sharing of knowledge and insights that happens in such groups). Many of us are overextended and fail to understand that just getting the group's logo on your profile does not in itself make one a skilled or knowledgeable person on the subject or an engaged group member. Nor will this help build our social capital.

Table 8.7 Reputation management

#	Rating	Continuously improving the process subsequent to the audit	Points
8.7.1	*****	How are we intending to further improve response(s) to warranty work (e.g., timeliness of repairs, supplying substitute products)?	0, 1, 2, or 3
8.7.2	*****	What steps are being taken to further refine our response(s) to requests on various social media platforms?	…
8.7.3	*****	Have we set objectives for further improving our active listener status within groups we are members of (e.g., employee on a LinkedIn group) (meaning one regularly contributes by writing a comment to other people's questions and contributions or threads started in a group), thereby contributing value to the group?	…
8.7.4	*****	Are we making a special effort to ensure other group members feel appreciated and comfortable by acknowledging other people's contributions (e.g., by replying to their comments, thereby keeping individuals engaged)?	
8.7.5	*****	Did we put together an itemized budget to spell out the resources needed to rectify the prioritized process problems for improving our reputation?	…

Note: Please remember that the clearer the guidance from the management review the more helpful it will be to the efforts taken for improvement of the process. For instance, what is adequacy or effectiveness in this context, or how we define and measure this, needs to be specified. What is acceptable performance or not must be understood

The total number of points can range from 0 to 3 for each item, which is then multiplied by the number of stars given, ranging from 1 to 5. The range of scores for each item is therefore 0 to 15, which is then multiplied by the number of questions. Accordingly, for the above table, the maximum score is 5 (questions) $\times$ 15 = 75

For more information about the calculations, scaling, and rationale, please see Table 5.1

8.8   Achieving a Better Customer Experience

Focusing on improving the customer experience before, during, and after the sale is critical to attaining and maintaining the reputation and image that we want for our brand and/or company.

Nevertheless, we also need to make sure that we do not just address and help those clients that shout the loudest on various social media channels. If we ignore the more quiet or subdued ones asking for help or warranty work, we are taking a risk that could backfire and severely hurt our reputation. To illustrate, a dissatisfied client is likely to talk to about nine people about the dissatisfying experience with our product or service staff. We want to ensure that we can use social media to help reduce this risk. We do not want our company be on the receiving end of too many negative sentiments. Just think about those negative Facebook updates on clients' wall or those tweets about our company.

In particular, we should document how we learn from resolving certain process problems as identified by the audit process. Client feedback is an important part of

Table 8.8 Achieving a better customer experience

#	Rating	Continuously improving the process subsequent to the audit	Points
8.8.1	*****	Do we learn systematically from process problems that customers complained about (e.g., as written in customer forums)?	0, 1, 2, or 3
8.8.2	*****	Are we systematically learning from the process issues that users raised in user forums (i.e., our platform or elsewhere)?	...
8.8.3	*****	Are we asking customers regularly for feedback both formally (e.g., survey) or informally (e.g., in an e-mail or during a conversation and record this for everybody to see!) to help us in further improving the output for clients?	...
8.8.4	*****	Do we have a way to collect customer feedback systematically, while reviewing such information carefully (e.g., qualitative process) to adjust the process during the subsequent period?	...
8.8.5	*****	Do we regularly adjust content to offer high quality customer experiences for fans and sales prospects?	...

Note: Please remember that the clearer the guidance from the management review, the more helpful it will be to the efforts taken for improvement of the process. For instance, what is adequacy or effectiveness in this context, or how we define and measure this, needs to be specified. What is acceptable performance or not must be understood

The total number of points can range from 0 to 3 for each item, which is then multiplied by the number of stars given, ranging from 1 to 5. The range of scores for each item is therefore 0 to 15, which is then multiplied by the number of questions. Accordingly, for the above table, the maximum score is 5 (questions) × 15 = 75

For more information about the calculations, scaling, and rationale, please see Table 5.1

this, particularly because a small minority will be willing to tell us about positive and negative experiences. If we get such feedback, we should use that information to improve customer service if feasible and practical. In other words, some people may also want more and be unreasonable. However, the majority are reasonable and probably justified in asking us to improve, and such feedback is valuable advice that must be taken into consideration.

Table 8.8 presents a few questions that can help us carefully use negative feedback to further improve customer experience or build on our strengths to provide better value to our clients.

8.9   Focusing on Solutions

Remember Section 3.2 entitled *Questions your CEO wants answered?* Now you need to be in position to review your audit data and have the answers to those questions US president Ronald Reagan was famous for wanting short memorandums that quickly informed him of the major issues in point form while you may use all the forms used here, give your boss a two-page synopsis to help them understand the most important facts quickly by providing them with an overview.

Table 8.9 is a template that uses the scale as presented in Table 3.1 to rank these challenges and problems accordingly. It provides your CEO with an indication of

Table 8.9 How to provide management with a synopsis of findings that are easy to grasp but detailed enough

Description of the problem	Describe by using example of the issue to be resolved	How these challenges can be resolved
Social media activities are not monitored closely enough during weekends and public holidays *Implementation*: Staff has know-how to take care of these issues	Concerns *Facebook posts* and *blog comments* If posted, not moderated until Monday morning. Negative comments on Facebook or inquiries not replied to until Monday	We have to monitor activities and reply not only during work days, but also during weekends and vacations. A schedule has to be set up-expense or overhead *Resources & Process*: Staff rotate the job to check before 10:00 AM and around 7:00 PM during a public holiday or a weekend day. Some compensation will be put in place (e.g., Internet access from home paid by company and time to be taken off as compensation) *Time*: Addressed within 2 weeks
Sometimes an employee authorized to tweet may send out a personal tweet via the corporate Twitter account instead of their own *Implementation*: Staff has know-how to take care of these issues	Concerns mistakes—*human error* Staff forget to log out of their private accounts on Twitter or Socialoomph.com. Result is a tweet about a beer bash intended for friends going to the corporate Twitter followers	Staff are sometimes too careless and forget that while they are logged in to some tool that permits the scheduling or immediate sending of tweets to various accounts, they could send the tweet to the wrong one. This could *damage the brand* *Resources & Process*: Staff have to be made aware of the importance of only logging in to the corporate account if they do social media work for the company right then tweets should be scheduled and checked and rechecked to make sure nothing embarrassing goes out. In turn, the risk of releasing an inadvertent tweet is significantly reduced *Time*: Addressed within 4 weeks (due to some people being on vacation)
To be continued	To be continued	To be continued

Note: To improve social media monitoring and execution, regular skills updating for staff is required. Color coding is taken from Table 3.1 to indicate the severity of the issue whether the challenge can be mastered (see Implementation) by using know-how available within the company. It also points out if some outsourcing might be needed or advisory services can help staff grapple with these issues faster and better.

Often, all that ends up in this table are the red-marked problems which are considered severe. There might be another table attached with challenges marked orange (critical) or yellow (essential) according to Table 3.1 that might also get done.

Table 8.9 also outlines resources needed (new staff or by assigning the task), as well as time requirements. Of course, you may want to use a different approach since you know your CEO better. Our experience has been that when we identify the problem (left column), we also need to provide the leadership with an example describing how the problem is manifesting (column 2 in Table 8.9). Focusing on operational issues also requires that we outline how we intend to resolve the problem (see column 3). Finally, a short description on what resources, including time, are required always gets top management's attention. Of course, these things need to be linked to the key drivers top management cares about. Unless you can show how this relates to getting more clients, reducing returns, etc. your top management or CEO may not care.

8.10 Conclusion

This section of the *CySoMAT* empowers you to systematically sift through social media audit data. In turn, you can then gain insights that allow you to put changes into place that will improve the process for next quarter.

What is critical here is that one does not just take the audit report as generated in Chapters 5–7, but goes to the trouble of analyzing these findings to use the insights gained to further improve the process.

In particular, we need to prioritize what we want to change and then present it to top management in a way that they can relate to (see Table 8.9). Once we get the okay to implement changes, including the budget and human resources needed to do so, we have to systematically track those changes. Tables 8.1, 8.2, 8.3, 8.4, 8.5, 8.6, 8.7, and 8.8 provide some pertinent questions that must be answered to ensure our space ship stays on course and saves fuel and time to deliver better customer service (i.e., arrive at the moon or wherever we want to go faster than the competition).

References

Gattiker, Urs E. (August 6, 2008). Brand versus reputation: Jeff Bezos, Richard Branson, Josef Ackermann and Pat Russo to the rescue. [Blog post - ComMetrics]. Retrieved January 15, 2012, from http://commetrics.com/?p=74

Gattiker, Urs, E. (September 7, 2011). 10 case studies: Is management on board. [Blog post - ComMetrics]. Retrieved February 29, 2012, from http://commetrics.com/?p=16342/

Gattiker, Urs E. (February 27, 2012). Twitter metrics: the ultimate list of tools. [Blog post - ComMetrics]. Retrieved February 29, 2012, from http://commetrics.com/?p=2089

Milkman, Katherine, L., Chugh, Dolly, Bazuerman, Max H. (2009). How can decision making be improved? Perspectives on Psychological Science, 4, 379–383.

Rick, Torben (March 11, 2011). Yet another social media failure [Blog post - Torben Rick writes]. Retrieved February 29, 2012, from http://www.torbenrick.eu/blog/social-media/yet-another-social-media-failure/

Chapter 9
Conclusions

Abstract Sixty-two percent of our workers can probably not make sense of the howling hurricane of noise and data they are getting. If some estimates are to be believed, the data deluge will continue to multiply grow by more than 40 times by 2020. This book discussed how this increasing amount of information can be used effectively when it comes to sCRM, social marketing, and customer engagement undertaken in any organization. Templates and checklists were provided to enable one to systematically assess the organization's activities using social media. In the conclusions, we outline some additional issues that you may have to address to stay ahead of the competition.

In the previous chapter, the focus was on using data obtained with the help of the audit to improve the process and further advance compliance, quality, and risk management. In this concluding chapter, the focus is on implementing and maintaining the process.

Governance is about how companies should be run in the context of society, as well as the law and best practice. Understanding and managing governance is an inherent part of the compliance process. *Without the proper governance policies and procedures in place, the company cannot achieve compliance with relevant regulations and laws.*

Governance describes the mechanisms an organization uses to ensure that its constituents follow its established processes and policies. *Governance is the primary means of maintaining oversight and accountability in a loosely coupled organizational structure.*

A *proper governance strategy implements systems to monitor and record what is going on, takes steps to ensure compliance with agreed policies, and provides for corrective action in cases where the rules have been ignored or misconstrued.*

Governance provides the structure and processes required for a company to be in compliance with new legislation. In fact as Figure 1.1 outlined, this book discussed the following issues:

- Introduction (Chapter 1)
- Cost analysis: Identifying direct and indirect costs (Chapter 2)
- Preparing for the social media audit (Chapter 3)
- Scope and focus of the social media audit (Chapter 4)
- Development and management (e.g., Facebook page) of the process (Chapter 5)
- Governance, compliance, and maintenance of the process (Chapter 6)
- Process evaluation and quality assurance (Chapter 7)
- Continuous improvement of the process (e.g., Twitter account) (Chapter 8)

These chapters provide you with the tools needed to go through these steps in a systematic way to assess where you are up to par and where your company or nonprofit organization must improve.

9.1   What an Audit Is Not

Addressing what the client's social media aim or expectation is surely not part of an audit, even though many audits might include it. When the accounting auditor comes by, do they ask what you expect from accounting? No, sir! They will check your situation and compare it to any regulations that apply to your company. Wherever discrepancies, compliance issues, risks, or mistakes are found, they will make a note and let you know at the end.

Of course, what *the purpose of using social media is in your company is an important factor.* However, *in the context of your social media audit, it is not.* You are *taking an inventory of what is already in place* and *the impact or effectiveness is of the process you audit.*

Of course, if the company changes its strategy this will affect the improvements you want to make, as outlined in Chapter 8. For instance, if they simply want to build their profile among bloggers within a certain niche or reach a particular audience, there are certain things that will need to be done. However, the *auditor will not tell you what you should do, but instead provide you with a snapshot of what is.*

9.2   Certain Risks Cannot Be Better Managed

As we pointed out in Chapter 5, in principle, *social media marketing must deal with three risks:*

1. *Lack of strategy* (see also Chapter 1), meaning the company has not clearly spelled out the purpose of using social media, nor how it intends to achieve what objectives.

2. *Overreliance on technology*, meaning the company relies on software tools such as Hubspot, Radian6, or My.ComMetrics.com to do their social media marketing. All three are excellent tools when used by trained people operating under the direction of a corporate strategy that outlines what goals must be accomplished (e.g., SMART (specific, manageable, actionable, relevant, trending) metrics including key drivers that measurement must focus on— Gattiker, 2012).

3. *Proliferation of social media marketing*, meaning different social media marketing efforts that blur brand image and may damage the firm's reputation (e.g., large firms average about 100 or more different social media accounts). This requires quality assurance with a social media audit, whereby processes are reviewed systematically. Results will show where the firm falls short, as well as where things can be improved and how (e.g., fewer Twitter accounts better focused).

Accordingly, *relying on Radian6 to solve your social media marketing issues is the similar to believing that a digital camera will solve your traditional marketing problems*. These are tools that, if used smartly, can help us a great deal, but they cannot solve underlying problems such as our inability to read or do mental math.

Nevertheless, defining *the purpose for using social media cannot become part of the audit work, nor can we include formulating strategy, such as setting goals to achieve*. These things are important and if not addressed, they at least pose a risk, if the lack does not set us up for failure. Moreover, actionable metrics that obviously link to key drivers such as higher customer retention must be included in our social media strategy's operationalization

Nonetheless, *audit results can and often do suggest changes for improvement*. Subsequent to the audit the organization might want to sift through the findings, then discuss them and suggest improvements. The latter may require that we adjust strategy and use of social media according to three factors that audit results indicate overall, namely:

1. *New opportunities* for starting certain activities or processes might have been identified during the audit (e.g., a new Facebook App, Google Plus, e-newsletter is preferred by a certain customer group) that if exploited could improve results.
2. *Changes in the business context* (e.g., economy is in a recession).
3. *Corporate strategy* changed when top management set new goals, such as higher growth target for the next couple of years for one or two markets.

These three possible events may necessitate a realignment of resources used and applied with social media. In turn, such work will help better engage with clients, and most importantly, help improve the customer experience. Of course, it is our challenge to show how the latter is linked to or positively influences key drivers (e.g., higher customer satisfaction, fewer returns or calls to the customer hotline) that link to higher sales.

9.3   Competitors and Best Practice

When reviewing the results of an audit and trying to decide where and how to improve, we *care about what our competitors do*. However, depending on our strategy, *we may walk a different path*.

For instance, a report points out that for US 2011 Inc. 500 companies, the use of blogs has declined, while new platforms including Facebook, LinkedIn, and Twitter now dominate. Moreover, the use of message boards, video blogging, podcasting, and MySpace in these companies is dropping (Barnes et al. 2012).

This is an important study. Nevertheless, just because these companies have dropped a bit in their use of blogs, as well as Second Life, is not in itself a reason to do the same, is it? Leaders discover and chart the way, they certainly do not follow like sheep. For instance, certain tools may be very good for you and your company due to your location. In Germany, Xing is certainly a better choice than LinkedIn for career-related matters. As well, managing/moderating a group can help increase your company's visibility with your German or Turkish clients.

Of course, if a competitor is very successful in doing something, the possibility of emulating it is an issue that warrants addressing. However, if Coca-Cola does something with success, this certainly does not necessarily result in Red Bull (the energy drink) following suit. Their target audiences may be similar but distinct enough to warrant very different approaches and use of social media.

The company may use the audit data collected in Chapters 3–7 to proceed and do a follow-up analysis addressing other issues, such as:

(a) What are our competitors doing in social media?
(b) What do they do similarly and what do they do differently (i.e., better or worse and why)?
(c) Could we emulate their successes?
(d) What platforms, content, and campaigns could work in our market niche and/or industry?
(e) What types of audiences are participating on these platforms and are they the ones we need and can reach there (i.e., do they want to engage with us there)?
(f) What strengths does the client have that can help effectively leverage the strengths of the company and platform to better engage with the target audience?
(g) What kinds of campaigns, content, and promotions must be implemented to reach the organization's strategy supported goals?

9.4   Final Words

Many people ignore that *the value of things is definitely determined by their rarity*. In economics 101, we learned it is all about *supply versus demand*. The more people share on ever more platforms using ever more channels, the less attention your target audience will pay to any individual image on Pinterest, post on Facebook, or shared entry on Google+. Somebody with five items posted on Facebook and 349 friends or passing acquaintances, would suggest the *increasingly diminished meaning such connections have*. We acquire these connections like trophies and sometimes cannot even remember that we are virtually connected with them when we meet them in person at a reception.

As communication becomes easier and the volume increases exponentially, the important thing is detecting whispers of useful information - quite the challenge. Companies need to be able to focus on a few channels, while producing the content that attracts enough people that want to share such content with their acquaintances in an ever changing set of social networks. For instance, Bebo came and left, so did Friendfeed - what about Facebook by 2014?

The templates presented in this book should help users better filter the onslaught of sound and information bites by putting the right processes in place. This will help extract meaning from the blizzard of information coming your way through various social media channels.

In such a howling hurricane of noise, we need to make sure that our organization is not only on board, but knows where it is going. It also wants to get the kind of participation that truly makes a difference in productivity, creativity, and collaboration. For one, we must be sure that social media in the workplace has the same characteristics as social media in our personal life:

1. *Strategy*—a clear, specific purpose that is linked to the corporate strategy.
2. *Technology*—designed around *user behavior* (intuitive, easy to use, training provided).
3. *Organization*—supported by new structures and practices as necessary (e.g., social media officer, privacy officer, risk management, and a tried and tested checklist for managing disaster, Gattiker, Urs E. August 11, 2010).
4. *Personal engagement*—catalyzed individual discretionary effort (get people and customers engaged, including top management, such as posting on the blog).

Strategy needs to have a purpose that helps build brand, but creates more than just buzz. Of course, watching TV at night may fulfill the purpose of allowing you to relax and/or be entertained. Similarly, engaging in discussions on certain groups may be for private purposes and to have a bit of fun (e.g., https://www.xing.com/net/businesskitchen/). However, if one does these things during work hours, they need to be linked to a clear and concise strategy. For instance, posting a white paper in a group could increase its exposure to more eyes and therefore by improve the company's visibility (e.g., as Salesforce does here: https://www.xing.com/net/smmetrics/free-resources-checklists-presentations-newsletters-sm-policies-436217/social-media-analysis-of-dld-12-39626700/39798583/#39798583). Similarly, doing an audit regarding the organization's social media activities is supposed to reveal strengths. Of course, it also shows weaknesses that warrant improvement to manage risks better and exploit opportunities more effectively. This strategy should be kept in mind when embarking on a social media audit.

Technology means that we have to use it in such a way that people can cope with it. For instance, we teach people how to pick up the phone and answer it properly in many organizations beyond just those working in a call center. Similarly, we expect people to use a signature box when sending out e-mail on their corporate account. But all these things require a certain level of training, and in some cases, learning by doing may be too risky a proposition.

The organization needs to put the structures and practices in place that enable it to manage these new channels effectively. This includes reducing the risk for a reputational disaster and improving customer relationship management (CRM).

In Germany, having a data protection officer is mandatory if the company has nine or more people with access to personal information (e.g., patient records, customer files, etc.) (Erstes Gesetz zum Abbau bürokratischer Hemmnisse insbesondere in der mittelständischen Wirtschaft, August 25, 2006). In this case, it is important that the data protection officer cannot be an employee from your IT department or IT security team. While this may not apply to your country, having such a position does help manage privacy risks better, particularly in conjunction with the use of social media, through which information may be divulged that could hurt the company.

We accept that everybody is in sales, so we should also accept that everybody uses social media. Put differently, if staff are not using certain platforms for work, they most probably do for private purposes. Examples include Google Reader, Hotmail, or Facebook and playing games online. As well, if one wants to engage, reader comments must be published even though they might ask tough questions. Most importantly, a qualified expert should provide a proper answer. If we are on social media, we should, of course, be authentic and this includes top management writing blog entries and participating. Customers want to hear their personal voice (e.g., video, podcast, or blog post) and not somebody from an advertising agency doing the job for the organization.

At this stage, I wish you all the best, and please, be social!

References

Barnes, Nora Ganim, and Lescault, Ava M. (February 2012). The 2011 Inc. 500 social media update: Blogging declines as newer tools rule. Center for Marketing Research, University of Massachusetts, Dartmouth. Retrieved Feburary 4, 2012, from. http://www.umassd.edu/cmr/stu diesandresearch/2011inc500socialmediaupdate/

Gattiker, Urs E. (August 11, 2010). Social media DO's and DON'Ts: 6 remedies for any emergency [Blog post - ComMetrics]. Retrieved January 15, 2012, from http://commetrics. com/?p=9456

Erstes Gesetz zum Abbau bürokratischer Hemmnisse insbesondere in der mittelständischen Wirtschaft (August 25, 2006) (First law for reducing bureaucratic constraints particularly for mid-sized businesses). Bundesgesetzblatt, Teil 1 (Artikel 1), G5702, Nr. 40, pp. 1970 – 1974. Retrieved January 15, 2012, from http://www.bgbl.de/Xaver/media.xav?SID = anonymous32 97385911577&tocf = Bundesanzeiger_BGBl_tocFrame&tf = Bundesanzeiger_BGBl_ mainFrame&qmf = Bundesanzeiger_BGBl_mainFrame&hlf = Bundesanzeiger_BGBl_ mainFrame&bk = Bundesanzeiger_BGBl&name = bgbl%2FBundesgesetzblatt%20Teil%20 I%2 F2006%2FNr.%2040%20vom%2025.08.2006%2Fbgbl106s1970.pdf

0 1341 1485944 7

CPSIA information can be obtained at www.ICGtesting.com
Printed in the USA
LVOW010357131212

311438LV00007B/245/P

9 781461 436027